Let It Snow!

IN PLASTIC CANVAS

Edited by Laura Scott

HOUSE of
WHITE
BIRCHES

PUBLISHERS
SINCE 1947

Let It Snow! in Plastic Canvas

Editor: Laura Scott
Associate Editor: Cathy Reef
Design Manager: Vicki Blizzard
Editorial Assistant: Katie Furtaw
Technical Editor: June Sprunger
Copy Editors: Michelle Beck, Mary Martin
Publications Coordinator: Tanya Turner
Technical Artists: Mitch Moss, Liz Morgan, Travis Spangler, Chad Summers

Photography: Andy Burnfield, Scott Campbell

Production Coordinator: Brenda Gallmeyer
Book and Cover Design: Jessi Butler
Graphic Artist: Pam Gregory
Production Assistants: Janet Bowers, Marj Morgan
Traffic Coordinator: Sandra Beres

Publishers: Carl H. Muselman, Arthur K. Muselman
Chief Executive Officer: John Robinson
Publishing Marketing Director: David McKee
Book Marketing Manager: Craig Scott
Product Development Director: Vivian Rothe
Publishing Services Manager: Brenda R. Wendling

Printed in the United States of America
First Printing: 2002
Library of Congress Number: 2001089864
ISBN: 1-882138-87-2

Every effort has been made to ensure the accuracy and completeness of the
instructions in this book. However, we cannot be responsible for human
error or for the results when using materials other than those specified in
the instructions, or for variations in individual work.

A Note From the Editor

None of us is ever too old to enjoy the wonder of snow. What is your favorite kind of snow? My daughter's favorite snow is a snow cone. My son's favorite snow is a snowball. My favorite? I love those big, fluffy snowflakes that fall ever so softly to the ground. I love the times when the weather is cold enough that those lovely snowflakes make a soft blanket on the ground in minutes. Even now as an adult with quickly growing-up children, one of my favorite winter activities is going out in one of those fluffy-flake snowfalls with a piece of black construction paper. Just last week I bought a set of three magnifying glasses to look at this year's snowflakes. The intricacy and beauty of those individual works of art never ceases to awe me!

This delightful book is filled with a different kind of work of art inspired by the beauty we enjoy and fun we have with the winter season.

As much as I love the warmer weather and flowers of summer, winter has a certain distinct and appreciated charm in my mind. During what other time of year can you munch on a frozen icicle treat untouched by human hands in its making? What other season affords us afternoons spent creating friendly, plump snowmen that will greet us with their cheery smiles for days or even weeks on end? During these chilly winter months, no one will look twice if you spend and extra hour or two every day stitching.

With this collection of delightful, snow-themed projects, you'll find many new projects just right for filling those cold winter afternoons. Wall decor, tissue box covers, table sets, centerpieces, baskets, ornaments and much, much more are sure to please you and those you love. Whether you make these projects to give as gifts, to sell, or to decorate your home, I'm confident they will bring you hours of stitching enjoyment throughout the year!

Warmest regards,

Laura Scott

Contents

- Chapter 3 -
Tabletop Decor

- Chapter 4 -
Christmas Joy

Deck the Walls

Fill your home with all the warmth and wonder of delightful plastic canvas wall and door decorations! Each will add a unique touch of wintry cheer to your home, bringing joy and beauty throughout the winter season!

LET IT SNOW

Snowman Towel Holder

Design by Jocelyn Sass & Karen White of Creatively Sassy

 ere's a winter helper that is both practical and decorative—a handy kitchen towel holder.

Skill Level
Beginner

Finished Size
8 inches W x 8⅜ inches H

Materials
- ½ sheet Darice Ultra Stiff 7-count plastic canvas
- Darice Nylon Plus plastic canvas yarn as listed in color key
- #16 tapestry needle
- 24 inches 1-inch-wide plaid ribbon
- 1⅝-inch sawtooth hanger
- Designer tacky glue

Instructions

1. Cut plastic canvas according to graph.

2. Stitch piece following graph, working uncoded area with white Continental Stitches.

3. Overcast mouth and hat edges with black; Overcast remaining edges with white.

4. Cut ribbon in half so there are two 12-inch lengths. Wrap one length around hat for hatband, gluing ends to backside. Tie remaining length in a bow, trimming ends as needed; glue to hat as in photo.

5. Glue sawtooth hanger to backside; allow to dry. Place kitchen towel through mouth opening. ✵

COLOR KEY	
Plastic Canvas Yarn	**Yards**
■ Black #02	30
■ Baby pink #10	1
☐ Powder pink #11	2
☐ Burnt orange #17	1
▨ Bittersweet #18	1
Uncoded area is white #01	
Continental Stitches	22
⟋ White #01 Overcasting	
Color numbers given are for Darice Nylon Plus plastic canvas yarn.	

Cut out

Snowman Towel Holder
53 holes x 54 holes
Cut 1

Snow-Happy Note Holder

Design by Judy Collishaw

Who can resist this handsome fellow? He's just right for leaving reminders for your family on the refrigerator!

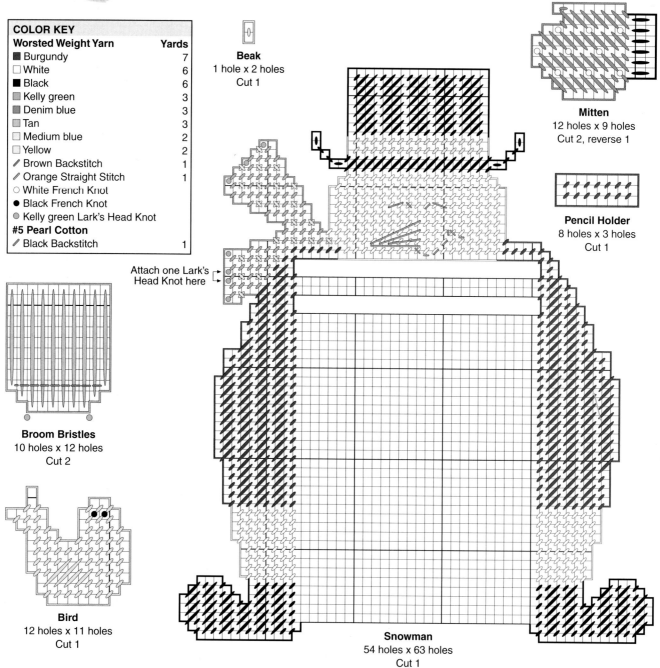

COLOR KEY

Worsted Weight Yarn	Yards
■ Burgundy	7
□ White	6
■ Black	6
▨ Kelly green	3
▨ Denim blue	3
▨ Tan	3
□ Medium blue	2
□ Yellow	2
✎ Brown Backstitch	1
✎ Orange Straight Stitch	1
○ White French Knot	
● Black French Knot	
◉ Kelly green Lark's Head Knot	
#5 Pearl Cotton	
✎ Black Backstitch	1

Attach one Lark's Head Knot here →

Beak
1 hole x 2 holes
Cut 1

Mitten
12 holes x 9 holes
Cut 2, reverse 1

Pencil Holder
8 holes x 3 holes
Cut 1

Broom Bristles
10 holes x 12 holes
Cut 2

Bird
12 holes x 11 holes
Cut 1

Snowman
54 holes x 63 holes
Cut 1

Skill Level
Beginner

Finished Size
8⅛ inches W x 10½ inches H

Materials
- 1 sheet 7-count plastic canvas
- Worsted weight yarn as listed in color key
- #5 pearl cotton as listed in color key
- #16 tapestry needle
- Pencil
- 4-inch x 6-inch notepad
- Low-temperature glue gun

Cutting & Stitching
1. Cut plastic canvas according to graphs.

2. Stitch broom bristles with tan following graph. Work brown Backstitches when tan stitching is completed. Overcast bottom edges from blue dot to blue dot, then Whipstitch wrong sides together along remaining edges.

3. Stitch pencil holder following graph. Overcast top and bottom edges; Whipstitch short edges together, forming a tube.

4. Stitch and Overcast remaining pieces following graphs, leaving center area of snowman unstitched as indicated. *Note: Some edges in notepad area will not be Overcast.*

5. Using full strands yarn through step 6, Straight Stitch orange nose on snowman's head and work white French Knots on mittens.

6. For scarf fringe, cut six 5-inch lengths of kelly green yarn. Attach one length each where indicated with a Lark's Head Knot. Fray ends and trim to 3/4-inch.

7. Use two strands black yarn to work French Knot eyes on bird. Work mouth and eyes of snowman with black pearl cotton.

Finishing
1. Use photo as a guide throughout finishing. Glue beak to bird, then glue bird to top of hat.

2. Glue pencil holder to snowman where indicated with blue line. With thumbs of mittens facing up, glue one mitten to each side of snowman, placing one mitten over pencil holder.

3. With eraser end up, insert pencil in pencil holder. Slip broom bristles over eraser.

4. Hang as desired. ❋

Snowmen Peg Rack

Design by Jocelyn Sass & Karen White of Creatively Sassy

hree dapper snowmen are lined up to add a friendly accent to your home! Orange wooden pegs give them delightful noses!

Skill Level

Beginner

Finished Size

13 inches W x 5¾ inches H

Materials

- 1 sheet Darice Ultra Stiff 7-count plastic canvas
- Uniek Needloft plastic canvas yarn as listed in color key
- Nylon plastic canvas yarn as listed in color key
- #16 tapestry needle
- 3 (1½-inch-long) wooden pegs
- Orange acrylic paint
- Paintbrush
- 2 (1⅜-inch) sawtooth hangers
- Designer tacky glue

Instructions

1. Cut plastic canvas according to graph, cutting out nose holes on front only. Back will remain unstitched.

2. Stitch front following graph, working uncoded areas with white Continental Stitches. Overcast nose edges with white.

3. Work French Knots when background stitching is completed, then Whipstitch front and back together following graph along outside edges and all remaining inside edges.

4. Paint wooden pegs orange; allow to dry. Glue pegs into nose holes; allow to dry.

5. For hanging, glue sawtooth hangers to backside; allow to dry. ✳

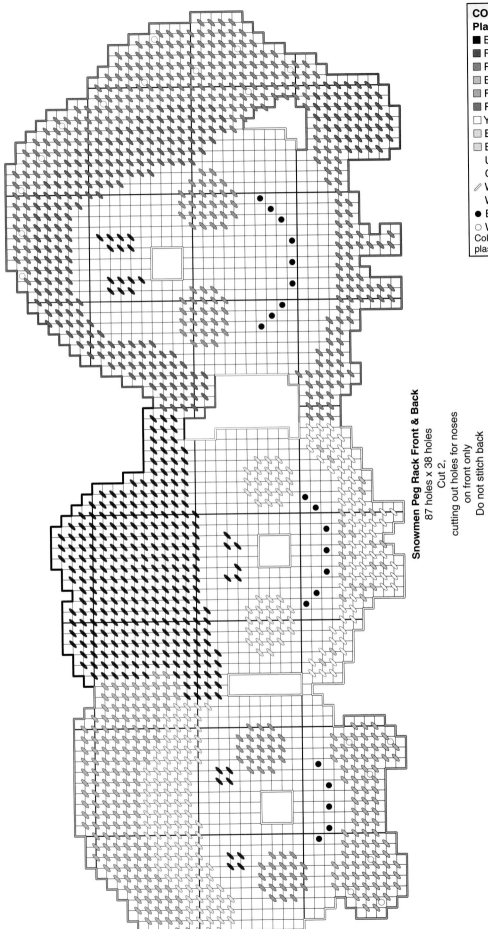

COLOR KEY

Plastic Canvas Yarn	Yards
■ Black #00	13
■ Red #01	6
■ Pink #07	2
■ Baby yellow #21	1
■ Forest #29	9
■ Royal #32	10
□ Yellow #57	3
■ Baby green	3
■ Baby pink	1
Uncoded areas are white #41	
Continental Stitches	17

⁄ White #41 Overcasting and
Whipstitching
● Black #00 French Knot
○ White #41 French Knot
Color numbers given are for Uniek Needloft
plastic canvas yarn.

Snowmen Peg Rack Front & Back
87 holes x 38 holes
Cut 2,
cutting out holes for noses
on front only
Do not stitch back

Snowman & Cardinals

Design by Kathleen Hurley

Capture the charm of two favorite winter characters with this pretty wall hanging picturing a friendly snowman entertaining his cardinal friends!

Skill Level

Intermediate

Finished Size

Approximately 13⅜ inches W x 15¾ inches H

Materials

- 3 sheets 7-count plastic canvas
- Coats & Clark Red Heart Classic worsted weight yarn Art. E267 as listed in color key
- #3 pearl cotton as listed in color key
- #16 tapestry needle
- Hot-glue gun

Instructions

1. Cut plastic canvas according to graphs (this page and pages 16 and 17).

2. Stitch and Overcast pieces following graphs, reversing one cardinal before stitching; work uncoded areas on hat below blue highlighted line, and on scarf below blue line and face with paddy green Continental Stitches. *Note: Uncoded area on head around face and above blue line should remain unstitched.*

3. When background stitching and Overcasting are completed, fill pompom area of hat with Loop Stitches, making loops ½-inch long. Cut each loop at center to form pompom.

4. Using black pearl cotton, Backstitch snowman's mouth; Straight Stitch thread lines on buttons. Add French Knots to snowman's eyes with white pearl cotton. Work French Knots for birds' eyes with light brown pearl cotton.

5. Using photo as a guide throughout, glue hat to snowman's head, covering unstitched area. Glue arm to body and body to base over unstitched area, making sure to align rows of white Slanted Gobelin Stitches.

6. Glue star to top of tree and to snowman's hand. Glue snowflakes to tree. Glue birds to snowman and to base.

7. Hang as desired. ❈

COLOR KEY	
Worsted Weight Yarn	**Yards**
□ White #1	47
■ Black #12	1
□ Yellow #230	4
▨ Orange #245	1
■ Mid brown #339	1
▨ Silver #412	8
■ Forest green #689	11
▨ Pink #737	1
■ Cherry red #912	21
Uncoded areas on scarf and below blue line on hat are paddy green #686 Continental Stitches	14
⁄ Paddy green #686 Overcasting	
#3 Pearl Cotton	
⁄ Black Backstitch	1
○ White French Knot	1
● Light brown French Knot	1
Color numbers given are for Coats & Clark Red Heart Classic worsted weight yarn Art. E267.	

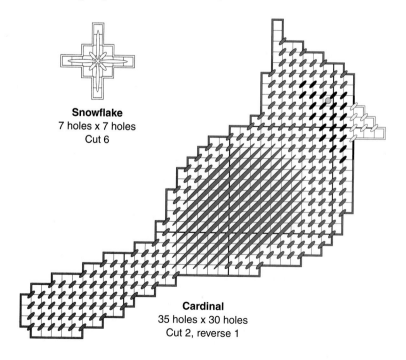

Snowflake
7 holes x 7 holes
Cut 6

Cardinal
35 holes x 30 holes
Cut 2, reverse 1

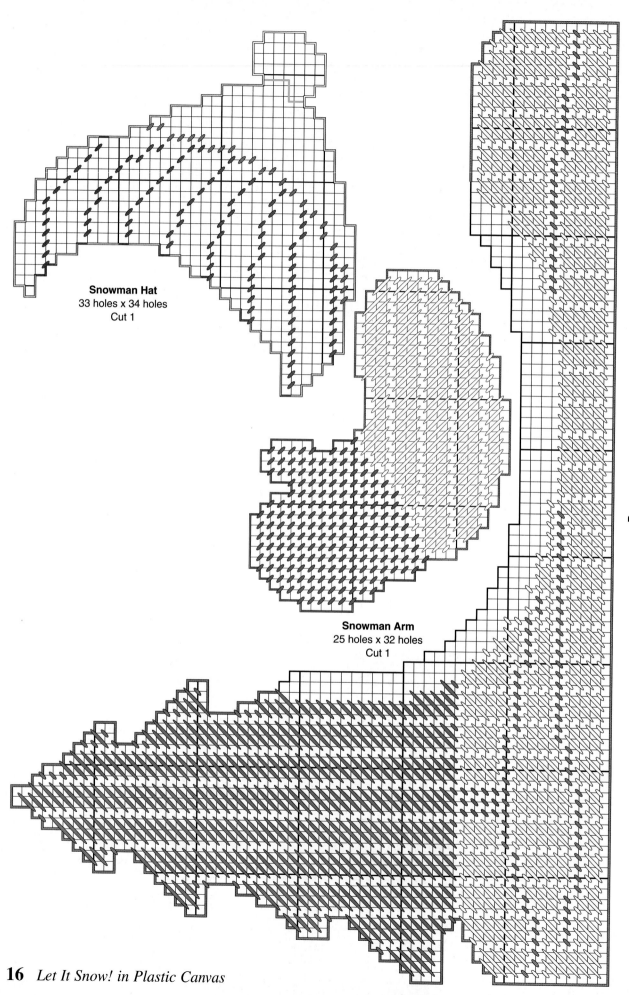

Snowman Hat
33 holes x 34 holes
Cut 1

Snowman Arm
25 holes x 32 holes
Cut 1

Base
90 holes x 58 holes
Cut 1

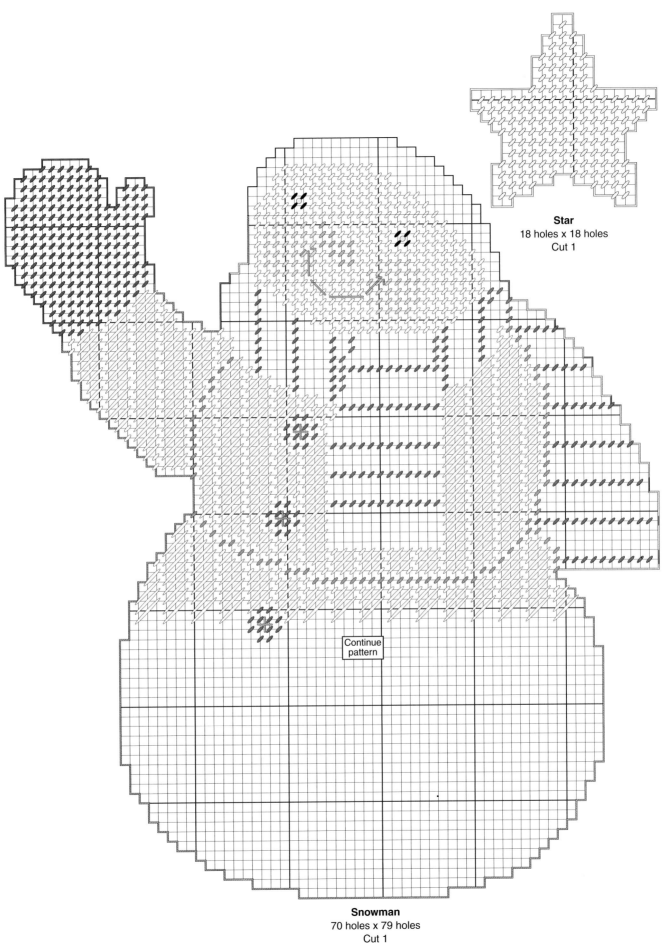

Star
18 holes x 18 holes
Cut 1

Snowman
70 holes x 79 holes
Cut 1

Continue
pattern

Cardinal Snow Scene

Design by Angie Arickx

Stitch this bright red cardinal against a pine bough for a lovely winter snow scene!

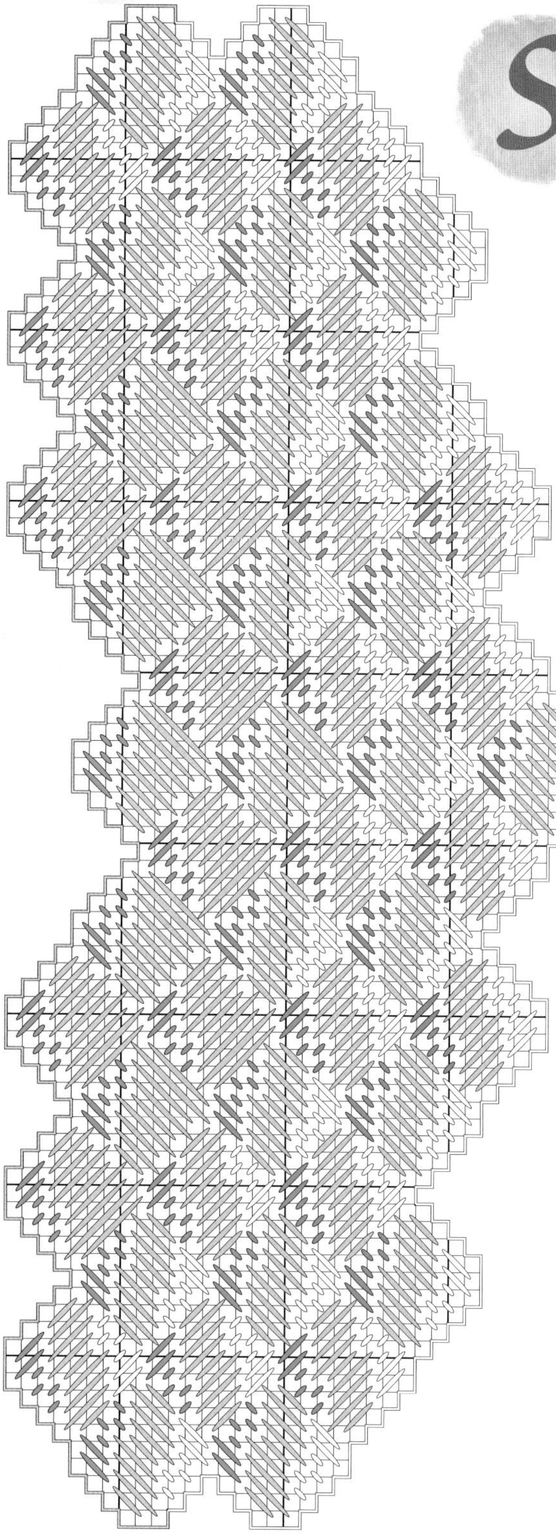

Greenery
89 holes x 37 holes
Cut 1

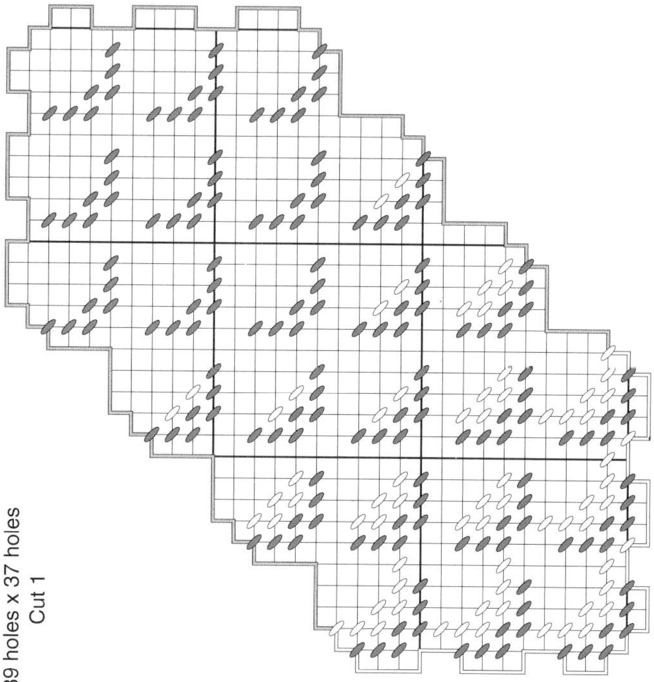

Pinecone
31 holes x 31 holes
Cut 3

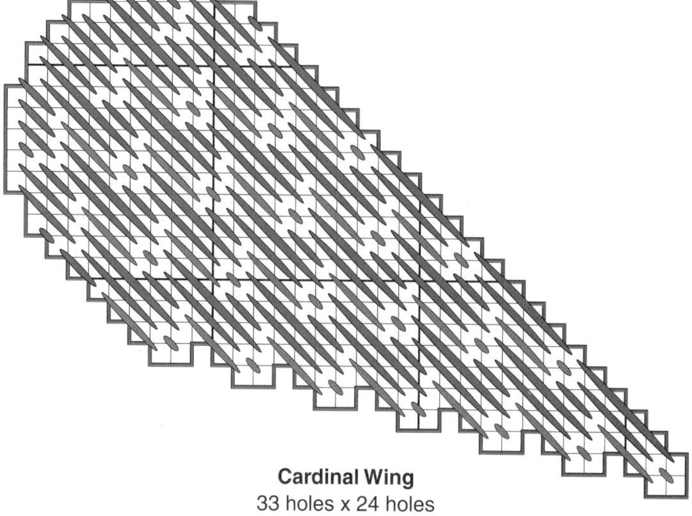

Cardinal Wing
33 holes x 24 holes
Cut 1

Skill Level

Beginner

Finished Size

13½ inches W x 12¾ inches H

Materials

- 2 sheets Uniek QuickCount 7-count plastic canvas
- Uniek Needloft plastic canvas yarn as listed in color key
- #16 tapestry needle
- Hot-glue gun

Instructions

1. Cut plastic canvas according to graphs (pages 18 and 22).

2. Stitch and Overcast pieces following graphs, working uncoded areas with camel Continental Stitches. Work black French Knot for eye on cardinal.

3. Using photo as a guide, glue wing to cardinal; glue cardinal to center top of greenery. Glue pinecones to bottom backside of greenery.

4. Hang as desired on wall, door or large wreath. ❋

COLOR KEY

Plastic Canvas Yarn	Yards
■ Black #00	1
■ Red #01	18
■ Burgundy #03	3
■ Tangerine #11	1
■ Brown #15	9
■ Christmas green #28	24
■ Forest #29	7
□ White #41	15
Uncoded areas are camel #43 Continental Stitches	19
✐ Camel #43 Overcasting	7
● Black #00 French Knot	

Color numbers given are for Uniek Needloft plastic canvas yarn.

Graphs continued on page 22

Snowman for Hire

Design by Kimberly A. Suber

Wouldn't you love to have this cheerful fellow around to help you shovel snow? With his bright hat and scarf and winning smile, he'll brighten any wintry day!

Skill Level
Beginner

Finished Size
13½ inches W x 13½ inches H

Materials
- 2 sheets Uniek QuickCount 7-count plastic canvas
- Worsted weight yarn as listed in color key
- #16 tapestry needle
- Hot-glue gun

Instructions
1. Cut plastic canvas according to graphs (pages 21 and 22).

2. Stitch and Overcast pieces following graphs, working uncoded background on sign with tan Continental Stitches. Continuing pattern given, work white Slanted Gobelin Stitches on body, arms and head, adjusting stitches to fill in completely around buttons, scarf and facial features.

3. When background stitching is completed, embroider eyebrows and mouth on snowman with 4 plies black and letters on sign with 2 plies black.

4. Using photo as a guide, glue shovel and sign to snowman's hands.

5. Hang as desired. ❋

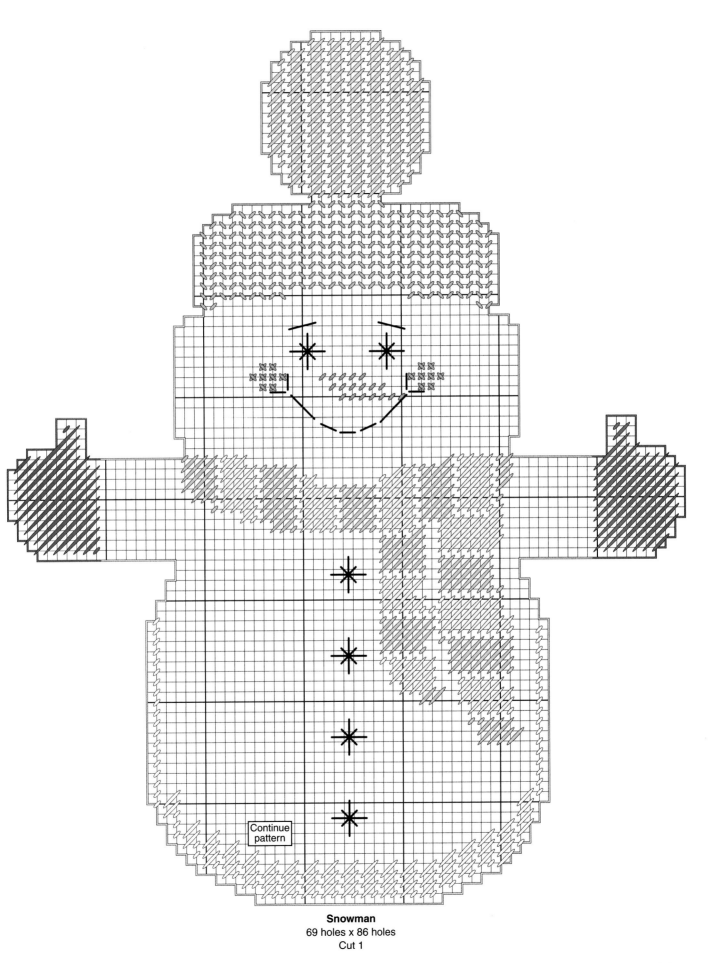

Snowman
69 holes x 86 holes
Cut 1

Continue pattern

COLOR KEY

Worsted Weight Yarn	Yards
☐ White	32
▨ Light orange	6
▨ Gray	6
☐ Yellow	5
▨ Bright pink	4
■ Purple	4
▨ Green	4
▨ Turquoise	3
■ Black	2
▨ Bright orange	1
▨ Watermelon	1
▨ Brown	1
■ Red	1
Uncoded background on sign is tan Continental Stitches	3
⁄ Light blue Overcasting	3
⁄ Black Backstitch and Straight Stitch	

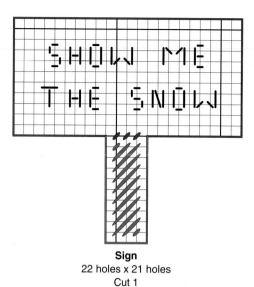

Sign
22 holes x 21 holes
Cut 1

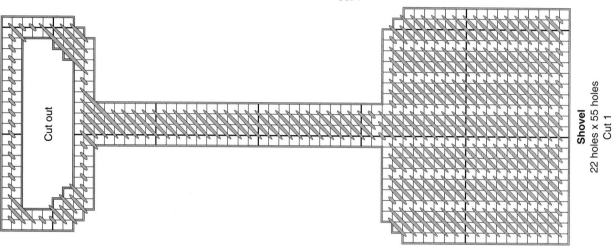

Shovel
22 holes x 55 holes
Cut 1

Cut out

Cardinal Snow Scene

Continued from page 19

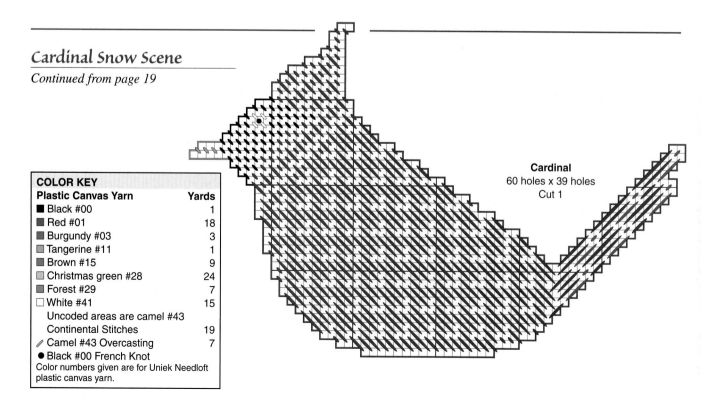

Cardinal
60 holes x 39 holes
Cut 1

COLOR KEY

Plastic Canvas Yarn	Yards
■ Black #00	1
■ Red #01	18
■ Burgundy #03	3
☐ Tangerine #11	1
■ Brown #15	9
▨ Christmas green #28	24
■ Forest #29	7
☐ White #41	15
Uncoded areas are camel #43 Continental Stitches	19
⁄ Camel #43 Overcasting	7
● Black #00 French Knot	

Color numbers given are for Uniek Needloft plastic canvas yarn.

Sledding Fun

Design by Kathy Wirth

Sitting on his candy-cane sled, this rosy-cheeked snowman is ready to zoom down the hill! All aboard!

Skill Level

Beginner

Finished Size

12¼ inches W x 10½ inches H

Materials

- 2 sheets 7-count plastic canvas
- Coats & Clark Red Heart Classic worsted weight yarn Art. E267 as listed in color key
- Metallic craft cord as listed in color key
- 20 (10mm) white pompoms
- #16 tapestry needle
- Hot-glue gun

Instructions

1. Cut plastic canvas according to graphs.

2. Following graphs throughout, Stitch front, working uncoded areas with white Continental Stitches. Do not stitch bars that are shaded blue. Stitch back, leaving areas indicated unworked.

3. When background stitching is completed, work Backstitches and

French Knots for eyes and mouth with 2 plies black.

4. Using full strands (4 plies) yarn, work emerald green Straight Stitches for stripes on candy-cane sled and jockey red Straight Stitches for nose and mitten cuff. Work lettering with sliver metallic craft cord.

5. On front, Overcast top edges of hill, sled and snowman from red dot to red

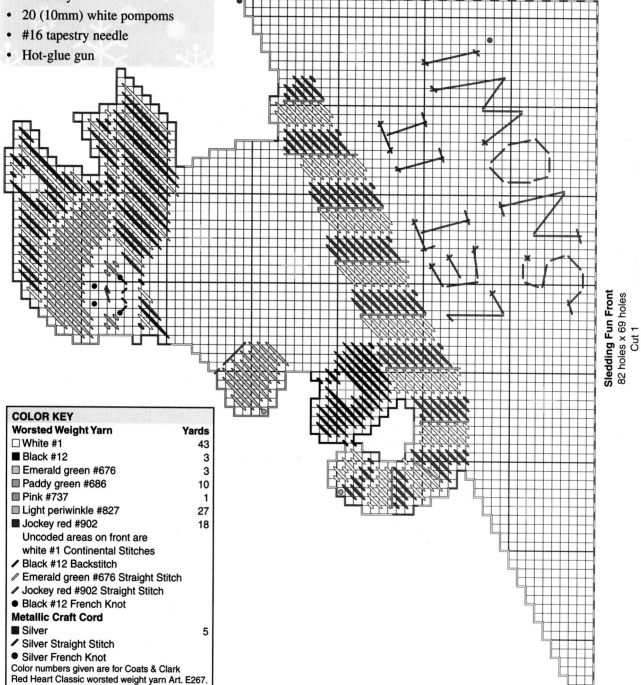

Sledding Fun Front
82 holes x 69 holes
Cut 1

COLOR KEY	
Worsted Weight Yarn	**Yards**
☐ White #1	43
■ Black #12	3
☐ Emerald green #676	3
☐ Paddy green #686	10
☐ Pink #737	1
☐ Light periwinkle #827	27
■ Jockey red #902	18
Uncoded areas on front are white #1 Continental Stitches	
╱ Black #12 Backstitch	
╱ Emerald green #676 Straight Stitch	
╱ Jockey red #902 Straight Stitch	
● Black #12 French Knot	
Metallic Craft Cord	
■ Silver	5
╱ Silver Straight Stitch	
● Silver French Knot	
Color numbers given are for Coats & Clark Red Heart Classic worsted weight yarn Art. E267.	

dot following graph, leaving bottom and right edges of hill unworked at this time.

6. Using photo as a guide through step 8, work four jockey red Turkey Loop Stitches at tip of hat; cut loops and fray ends. Attach silver metallic cord

from blue dot on mitten to blue dot on sled, securing ends on backside.

7. Place front on back, matching bottom edge and lower portion of right edge. Whipstitch together with alternating stitches of white and jockey

red, Overcasting remaining edges of back while Whipstitching. Glue loose Overcast edges of front to back.

8. Glue white pompoms to unstitched areas on front and back.

9. Hang as desired. ❈

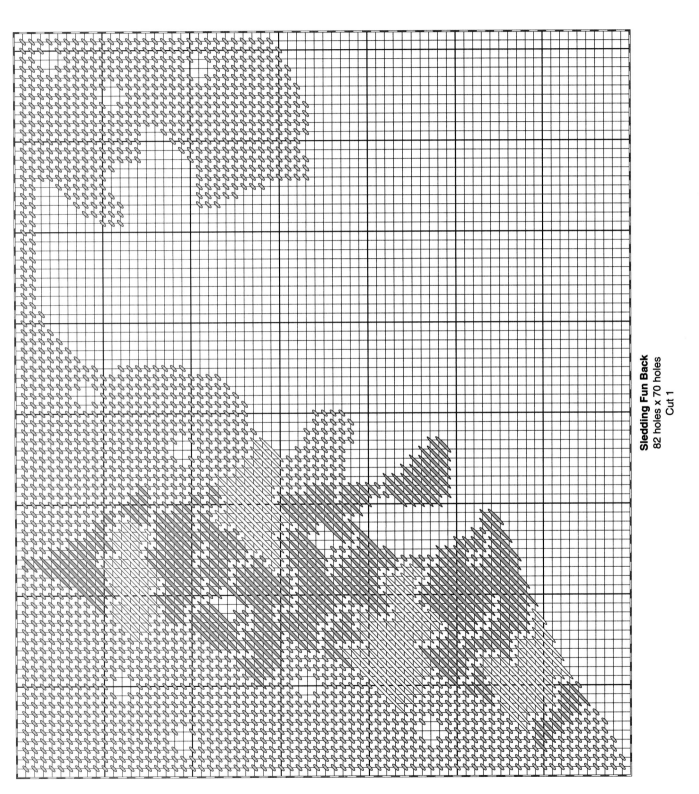

Sledding Fun Back
82 holes x 70 holes
Cut 1

Juggling Snowman

Design by Kathy Wirth

 Even snowmen have talent! This adorable snowman is juggling seven snowballs at one time!

Skill Level

Beginner

Finished Size

5⅝ inches W x 5⅛ inches H

Materials

- ¼ sheet white 10-count plastic canvas
- Coats & Clark Red Heart Classic worsted weight yarn Art. E267 as listed in color key
- #18 tapestry needle
- 7 (10mm) white pompoms
- 18-inches 18-gauge white cloth-wrapped stem wire
- Golf pencil or large nail
- Magnet (optional)
- Hot-glue gun

Project Note

For help in threading needle, first fold a small piece of paper over yarn end.

Instructions

1. Cut plastic canvas according to graph.

2. Stitch piece following graph, working black yarn stitches last. When background stitching is completed, Backstitch mouth with 2 plies black.

3. To curl wire, wrap wire around golf pencil or large nail. Using photo as a guide, glue ends behind mittens; glue pompoms to wire. ❄

COLOR KEY	
Plastic Canvas Yarn	**Yards**
☐ White #1	5
■ Black #12	4
☐ Sea coral #246	1
▨ Medium coral #252	1
☐ Blue jewel #818	3
▨ True blue #822	4
✦ Black #12 Backstitch	
Color numbers given are for Coats & Clark Red Heart Classic worsted weight yarn Art. E267.	

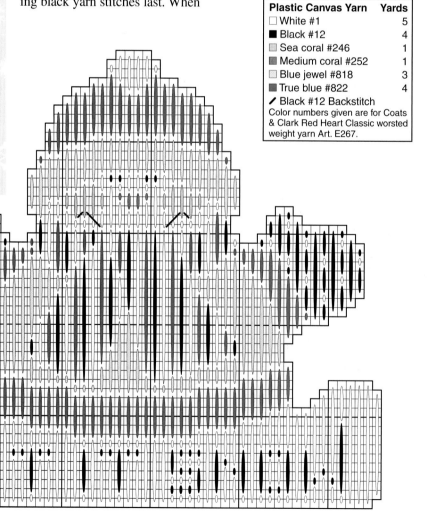

Juggling Snowman
56 holes x 50 holes
Cut 1

Snowman Quilt

Design by Joan Green

titch a patchwork of wintry charm with this pretty miniature quilt!
Pretty shades of teal, blue and lavender make it picture-perfect!

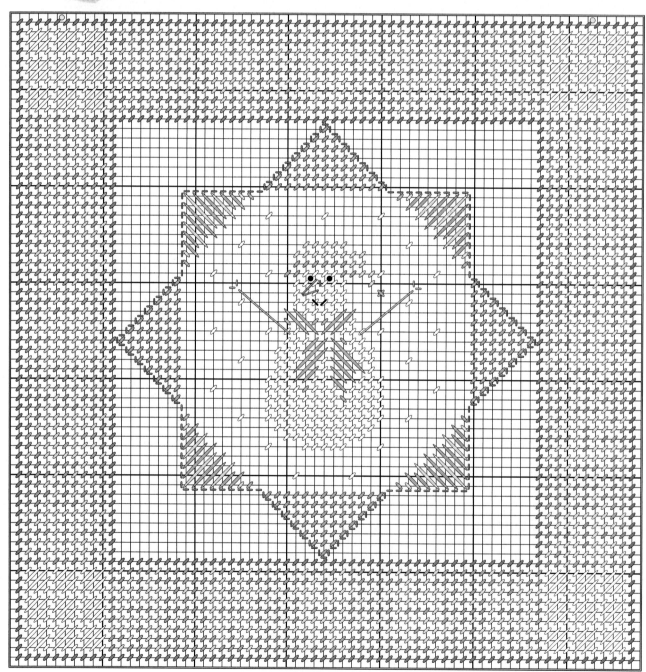

Snowman Quilt
68 holes x 68 holes
Cut 1

Skill Level

Intermediate

Finished Size

Approximately 6⅞ inches W x 10¾ inches H including hanger

Materials

- ½ sheet 10-count plastic canvas
- DMC 6-strand embroidery floss as listed in color key
- #18 tapestry needle
- 18 inches 18-gauge pearlized gold #150102S Fun Wire from Amaco
- 4 Mill Hill Products gold star ceramic buttons #86016 from Gay Bowles Sales Inc.
- Sewing needle and white sewing thread or 6-strand embroidery floss
- Pencil
- Fabric glue (optional)

Instructions

1. Cut plastic canvas according to graph.

2. Following graph through step 6 and using two full strands (12 plies) floss through step 5, work dark navy blue Continental Stitches along edges and along inside edge of border.

3. Work white Scotch Stitches in corners. Work very light plum and very dark blue Long Stitches in corners of center snowman quilt block.

4. Stitch remainder of center block, working uncoded background around snowman with very dark blue Continental Stitches. Work corners of block under center snowman block with dark seagreen Continental Stitches.

5. Work border strips between white corners. Work remaining uncoded area around two center blocks with light seagreen Continental Stitches. Overcast with dark seagreen.

6. When background stitching is completed, use 12 plies floss to embroider medium coral nose and light tan arms and hands. Use 6-plies black to Backstitch mouth and work French Knot eyes, and 6 plies dark navy blue to Backstitch around corners of two

center quilt blocks.

7. Using sewing needle and white sewing thread or floss, center and sew gold star buttons to four white corners, knotting ends and weaving in securely on backside.

8. For hanger, wrap wire around pencil to coil. Glue ends to top backside or thread ends from front to back through holes indicted, wrapping wire around itself or coiling slightly on backside to secure. ❊

COLOR KEY

6-Strand Embroidery Floss	Yards
☐ White	20
◼ Dark navy blue #823	24
☐ Very dark blue #824	54
◼ Dark seagreen #958	42
☐ Light seagreen #964	38
◼ Very light plum #3608	18
Uncoded background around snowman is very dark blue #824 Continental Stitches	
Uncoded areas around two center quilt blocks are light seagreen #964 Continental Stitches	
✎ Black #310 Backstitch	1
✎ Medium coral #350 Backstitch	1
✎ Light tan #437 Backstitch and Straight Stitch	1
✎ Dark navy blue #823 Backstitch	
● Black #310 French Knot	
○ Attach wire hanger	

Color numbers given are for DMC 6-strand embroidery floss.

Snowman With Heart

Design by Susan D. Fisher

Elegant writing on a bright red heart
will add charm to your country home!

Skill Level

Beginner

Finished Size

9½ inches W x 6½ inches H

Materials

- ½ sheet 7-count plastic canvas
- Coats & Clark Red Heart Classic worsted weight yarn Art. E267 as listed in color key
- #16 tapestry needle
- 2½-inch white pompom
- Hot-glue gun
- 12 inches ¼-inch-wide white ribbon

Instructions

1. Cut plastic canvas according to graphs.

2. Stitch pieces following graphs, working uncoded background on heart with cherry red Continental Stitches and uncoded area on snowman with white Continental Stitches.

3. Overcast pieces following graphs,

leaving edges between arrows on arms and on shoulders of snowman unworked at this time.

4. Work lettering and snowflakes on heart. Work eyes, nose, mouth, holly berries and holly leaves on snowman.

5. Using white, Whipstitch arms to shoulders on snowman from arrow to arrow.

6. Using photo as a guide throughout, glue pompom (for snowball) to snowman body, placing hands over pompom. Glue snowman to right side of heart.

7. For hanger, glue ends of ribbon to top backside of heart where indicated with arrows. ✳

COLOR KEY

Worsted Weight Yarn	Yards
☐ White #311	8
■ Black #312	2
▨ Cherry red #319	19
☐ Emerald green #676	2

Uncoded area on snowman is white #311 Continental Stitches
Uncoded background on heart is cherry red #319 Continental Stitches

	Yards
⁄ Paddy green #686 Backstitch and Overcasting	5
⁄ Orange #245 Straight Stitch	1
⁄ White #311 Straight Stitch	
⁄ Emerald green #676 Backstitch and Straight Stitch	
● Black #312 French Knot	
● Cherry red #319 French Knot	

Color numbers given are for Coats & Clark Red Heart Classic worsted weight yarn Art. E267.

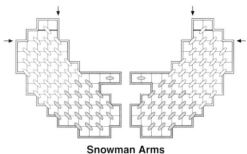

Snowman Arms
10 holes x 11 holes each
Cut 1 set

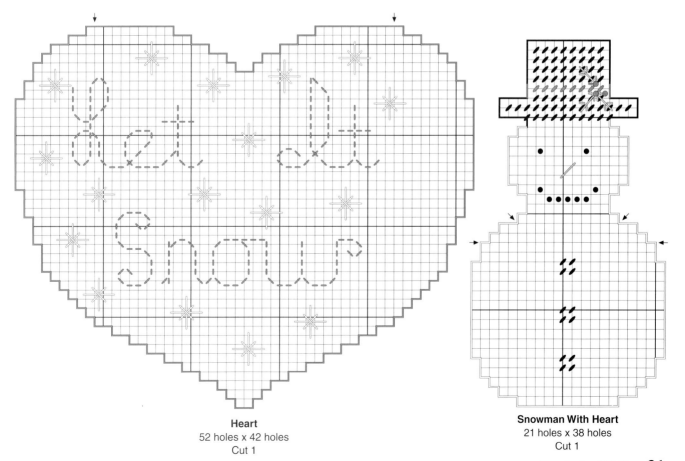

Heart
52 holes x 42 holes
Cut 1

Snowman With Heart
21 holes x 38 holes
Cut 1

Snow Family

Designs by Ronda Bryce

ress up your fireplace mantel with this friendly snowman family, including Mom, Dad and Baby Snowman!

Skill Level

Intermediate

Finished Size

Dad: 4¼ inches W x 8⅝ inches H, excluding hanger

Mom: 4¼ inches W x 8⅝ inches H, excluding hanger

Baby: 3½ inches W x 5⅝ inches H x 2⅛ inches D, excluding hanger

Materials

- 1 sheet 7-count plastic canvas
- 4 (4-inch) Uniek QuickShape plastic canvas radial circles
- 2 (3-inch) Uniek QuickShape plastic canvas radial circles
- Coats & Clark Red Heart Classic worsted weight yarn Art. E267 as listed in color key
- Coats & Clark Red Heart Super Saver worsted weight yarn Art. E300 as listed in color key
- #16 tapestry needle
- 2 (1¾-inch to 2-inch) papier-mâché carrots with attached paper carrot top
- ½-inch iridescent pompoms: 7 pink, 1 blue, 1 yellow
- 4 (5mm) white pompoms
- 14 (8mm) black faceted beads
- 2¼-inch doll eyeglasses #7281 from Fibre-Craft Materials Corp.
- 22mm x 45mm pink, blue or yellow pacifier bead from Darice
- Sewing needle and matching sewing thread
- Pliers (optional)

Cutting & Stitching

1. Cut dad and mom heads and hats from 4-inch plastic canvas radial circles, and baby head and hat from 3-inch plastic canvas radial circles according to graphs (this page and pages 34 and 37), cutting away gray areas.

2. Cut scarves, hatbands and receiving blanket from regular 7-count plastic canvas according to graphs (pages 34 and 37).

3. Stitch and Overcast pieces following graphs, leaving edges at center holes on heads, at white fringe area on scarves and at sides on receiving blanket unstitched. Work orange French Knot nose on baby head.

Finishing

1. Use photo as a guide throughout finishing. Insert pacifier in center hole of baby head.

2. Using sewing needle and matching sewing thread through step 7, sew hatbands to hats, then sew hats to heads. Sew scarves to corresponding heads.

3. Attach black beads for eyes on all heads, and to dad and mom heads for mouths.

4. For dad's mustache, attach four white pompoms above mouth. Attach two pink pompoms to each head for cheeks. Attach blue, pink and yellow pompoms to center top of hat with matching color.

5. Wrap receiving blanket around bottom third of baby head, overlapping edges. Stitch overlap together, then stitch blanket to head.

6. For carrot noses, insert carrot top through center hole on dad and mom heads. Spread top apart and sew to backside to secure.

7. Using pliers, if desired, straighten ends of temples on eyeglasses, then insert through holes on head. Bend temples down on backside and tack in place.

8. For dad's hanger, cut desired length of light blue yarn. Thread ends from front to back through two holes at top of hat; tie ends together in a knot on backside. Repeat for remaining ornaments, using petal pink for mom's hanger and pale yellow for baby's hanger. ✳

COLOR KEY	
Worsted Weight Yarn	**Yards**
☐ White #311	32
☐ Pale yellow #322	10
▨ Petal pink #373	12
☐ Light blue #381	13
■ Royal #385	9
▨ Grenadine #730	3
● Orange #245 French Knot	1
Color numbers given are for Coats & Clark Red Heart Classic worsted weight yarn Art. E267 and Super Saver worsted weight yarn Art. E300.	

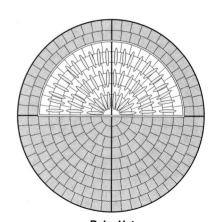

Baby Hat
Cut 1,
cutting away gray area

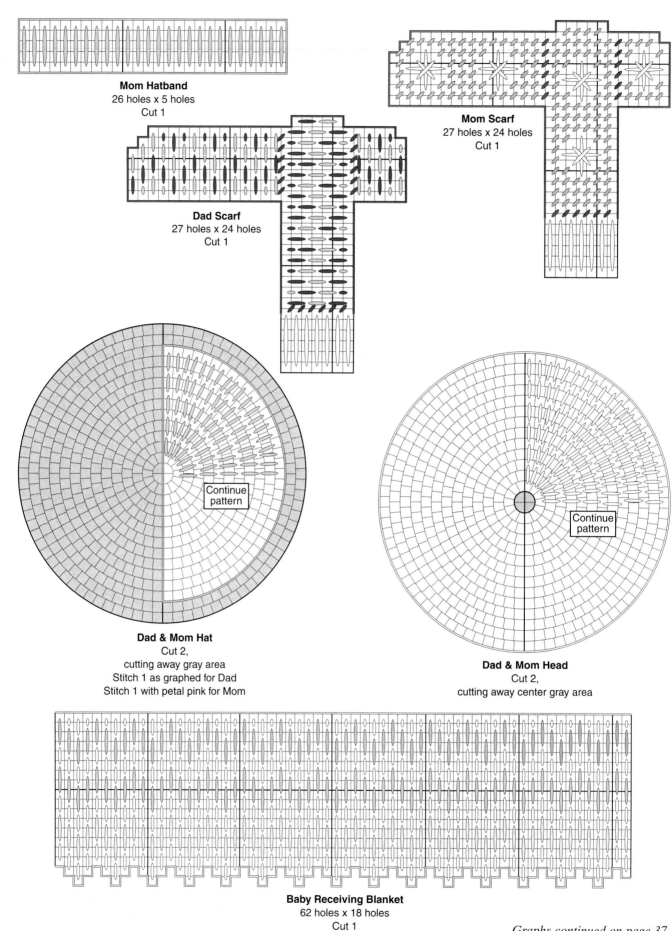

Mom Hatband
26 holes x 5 holes
Cut 1

Mom Scarf
27 holes x 24 holes
Cut 1

Dad Scarf
27 holes x 24 holes
Cut 1

Continue
pattern

Continue
pattern

Dad & Mom Hat
Cut 2,
cutting away gray area
Stitch 1 as graphed for Dad
Stitch 1 with petal pink for Mom

Dad & Mom Head
Cut 2,
cutting away center gray area

Baby Receiving Blanket
62 holes x 18 holes
Cut 1

Graphs continued on page 37

Doves in Pine

Design by Kristine Loffredo

ang peaceful doves sitting in pines for a gentle nature view that will soothe your soul! Photo on next page.

Skill Level

Intermediate

Finished Size

12 inches W x 10⅞ inches H

Materials

- 2 sheets Uniek QuickCount 7-count plastic canvas
- Uniek Needloft plastic canvas yarn as listed in color key
- Uniek Needloft metallic craft cord as listed in color key
- #16 tapestry needle
- Craft glue or hot-glue gun

Instructions

1. Cut plastic canvas according to graphs (this page and page 37), cutting away gray areas on pine branch oval.

2. Stitch pieces following graphs, working uncoded branches with brown Cross Stitches and leaving bar indicated with blue line on each dove unworked at this time. *Note: Top of oval and middle section of bow will remain unstitched.*

3. When background stitching is completed, work brown French Knots for doves' eyes.

4. Overcast bow knot. Overcast bow, leaving ends unworked. With wrong sides facing, fold ends of bow to center and tack in place with Christmas red. Glue bow knot over ends at center of bow.

5. Overcast pine branch oval and birds. Using white throughout, Overcast wings around sides and bottom edges from dot to dot, then Whipstitch top edge of each wing to unstitched bar on corresponding bird.

6. Using photo as a guide, glue bird A to branch at center left side of oval. Glue bird B to branch on center right side.

7. Glue or tack bow in place over unstitched area at center top of oval.

8. Hang as desired. ❈

COLOR KEY	
Plastic Canvas Yarn	**Yards**
■ Christmas red #02	7
■ Christmas green #28	19
■ Royal #32	11
□ White #41	11
■ Camel #43	1
Uncoded areas are brown #15 Cross Stitches	20
✎ Brown #15 Overcasting	
● Brown #14 French Knot	
Metallic Craft Cord	
✎ Gold #55001 Overcasting	4
Color numbers given are for Uniek Needloft plastic canvas yarn and metallic craft cord.	

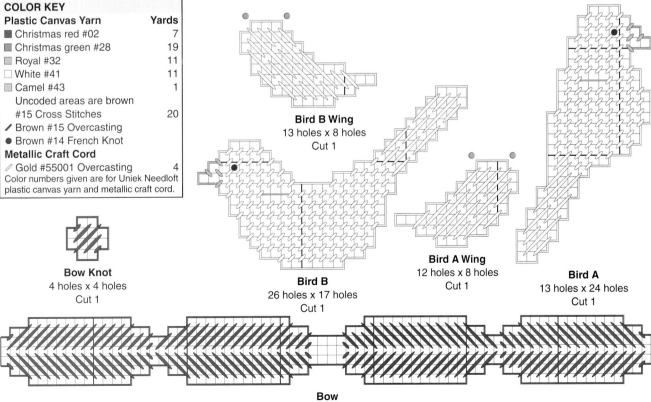

Bow Knot
4 holes x 4 holes
Cut 1

Bird B Wing
13 holes x 8 holes
Cut 1

Bird B
26 holes x 17 holes
Cut 1

Bird A Wing
12 holes x 8 holes
Cut 1

Bird A
13 holes x 24 holes
Cut 1

Bow
70 holes x 7 holes
Cut 1

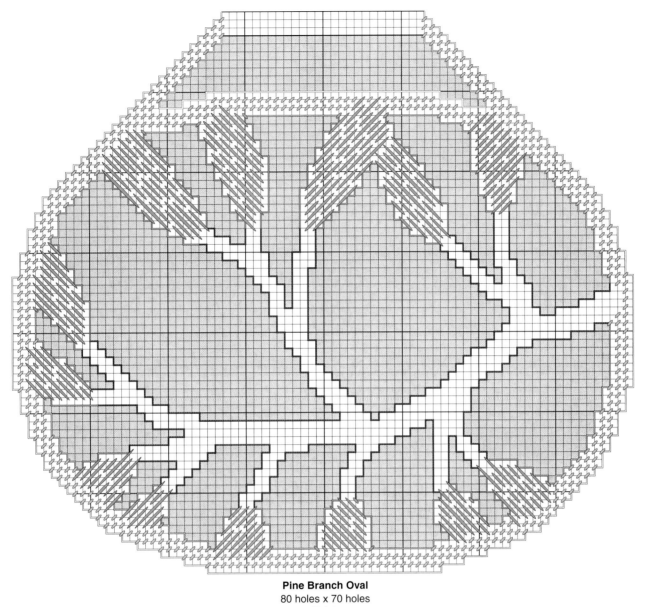

Pine Branch Oval
80 holes x 70 holes
Cut 1,
cutting away gray areas

Snow Family

Continued from page 34

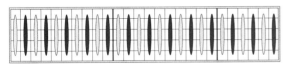

Dad Hatband
26 holes x 5 holes
Cut 1

Baby Hatband
16 holes x 2 holes
Cut 1

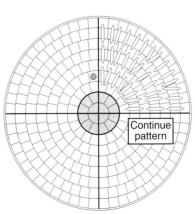

Continue
pattern

Baby Head
Cut 1,
cutting away center gray area

Snowflake Reflections

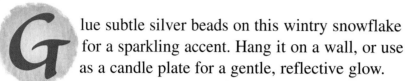

Design by Joan Green

G lue subtle silver beads on this wintry snowflake
for a sparkling accent. Hang it on a wall, or use
as a candle plate for a gentle, reflective glow.

Skill Level

Beginner

Finished Size

10½ inches W x 10½ inches H

Materials

- 1 sheet 7-count plastic canvas
- Coats & Clark Red Heart Super Saver worsted weight yarn Art. E300 as listed in color key
- #16 tapestry needle
- 88 (3mm) round silver beads
- 5-inch round flat mirror
- Sewing needle and white sewing thread
- Sawtooth hanger
- Fabric glue

Instructions

1. Cut plastic canvas according to graph.

2. Stitch piece following graph, working uncoded areas with Windsor blue Continental Stitches.

3. When background stitching is completed, work French Knots with 2 plies white. Overcast inside and outside edges with Windsor blue.

4. With sewing needle and white sewing thread, attach silver beads where indicated on graph; knot ends and weave in to secure.

5. Run a substantial bead of fabric glue on backside around center opening. Center mirror and press into glue. Place a heavy object on top of mirror while glue is drying.

6. Glue sawtooth hanger to top backside. ✳

COLOR KEY	
Worsted Weight Yarn	**Yards**
☐ White #311	22
Uncoded areas are Windsor blue #380 Continental Stitches	28
╱ Windsor blue #380 Overcasting	
○ White #311 French Knot	
● Attach 3mm silver bead	
Color numbers given are for Coats & Clark Red Heart Super Saver worsted weight yarn Art. E300.	

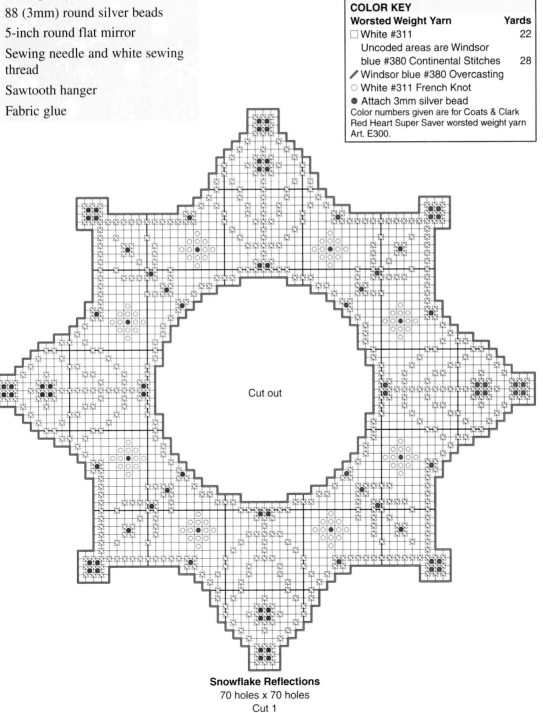

Snowflake Reflections
70 holes x 70 holes
Cut 1

Snowflake Joy

Design by Joan Green

 etailed lettering with metallic silver yarn transforms an ordinary wall hanging into a lovely holiday accent piece!

COLOR KEY

Worsted Weight Yarn	Yards
☐ White #311	7
▨ Lilac #353	26
■ Periwinkle #2347	26
Uncoded areas on letters are periwinkle #2347 Continental Stitches	
✐ White #311 Backstitch and Straight Stitch	
✐ Soft navy #387 Backstitch	4
¹/₈-Inch Metallic Needlepoint Yarn	
☐ Silver #PC2	3
¹/₁₆-Inch Metallic Needlepoint Yarn	
◉ Silver #PM52 French Knot	5

Color numbers given are for Coats & Clark Red Heart Super Saver worsted weight yarn Art. E300 and Kids worsted weight yarn Art. E711, and Rainbow Gallery Plastic Canvas 7 and Plastic Canvas 10 Metallic Needlepoint Yarn.

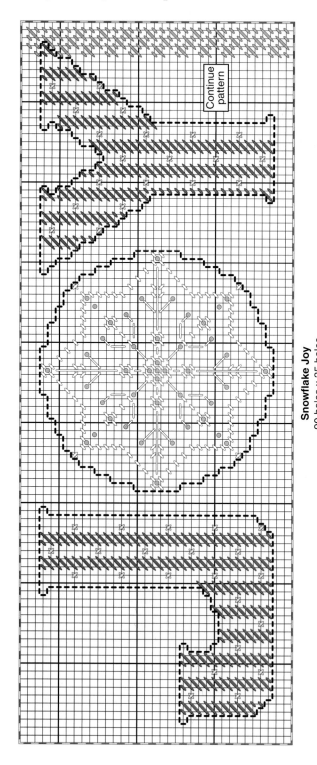

Snowflake Joy
90 holes x 35 holes
Cut 1

Skill Level

Intermediate

Finished Size

13½ inches W x 5¼ inches H

Materials

- ½ sheet 7-count plastic canvas
- Coats & Clark Red Heart Super Saver worsted weight yarn Art. E300 as listed in color key
- Coats & Clark Red Heart Kids worsted weight yarn Art. E711 as listed in color key
- #16 tapestry needle
- Sawtooth hanger

- ⅛ inch-wide Plastic Canvas 7 Metallic Needlepoint Yarn by Rainbow Gallery as listed in color key
- 1/16 inch-wide Plastic Canvas 10 Metallic Needlepoint Yarn by Rainbow Gallery as listed in color key
- Royal blue adhesive-backed Presto felt by Kunin Felt
- Fabric glue

Instructions

1. Cut plastic canvas according to graph.

2. Stitch piece following graph, working uncoded areas on letters with periwinkle Continental Stitches.

3. When background stitching is completed, work Backstitches and Straight Stitches on snowflake (letter "O") with 4 plies white. Work French knots with silver 1/16-inch metallic needlepoint yarn. Using 2 plies soft navy, work Backstitches around all letters.

4. Starting at bottom center of design, Overcast edges using periwinkle yarn worked in every other hole all around edge. Using silver ⅛-inch metallic needlepoint yarn, Overcast edges in remaining holes to give a striped look.

5. Cut felt to cover backside, then adhere. Center and glue sawtooth hanger to top backside. ✳

Snowflake Cornices

Design by Angie Arickx

COLOR KEY

Plastic Canvas Yarn	Yards
■ Royal #32	90
□ White #41	60

Color numbers given are for Uniek Needloft plastic canvas yarn.

Give your home an inviting winter appearance with the cool white of the season's first snowfall.

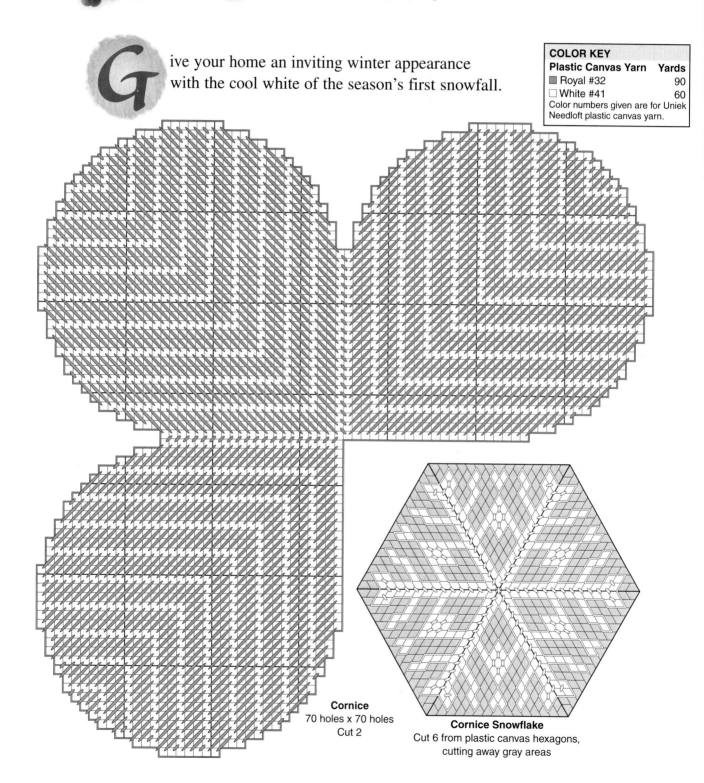

Cornice
70 holes x 70 holes
Cut 2

Cornice Snowflake
Cut 6 from plastic canvas hexagons,
cutting away gray areas

Skill Level
Intermediate

Finished Size
10½ inches W x 10½ inches H

Materials
- 2 sheets Uniek QuickCount 7-count plastic canvas
- 6 (5-inch) Uniek QuickShape plastic canvas hexagons
- Uniek Needloft plastic canvas yarn as listed in color key
- #16 tapestry needle
- Hot-glue gun

Instructions
1. Cut plastic canvas according to graphs, cutting away gray areas on hexagon for snowflakes.

2. Stitch and Overcast pieces following graphs.

3. Using photo as a guide, center and glue one snowflake to each circle on cornices.

4. Attach above door corners as desired. ✳

Snowman Suncatcher

Design by Susan Leinberger

Clear beads suspended on transparent thread will capture sunbeams as they surround this enchanting project.

Skill Level
Intermediate

Finished Size
9⅛ inches W x 10½ inches H

Materials
- 1 sheet Uniek QuickCount 7-count plastic canvas
- Uniek Needloft plastic canvas yarn as listed in color key
- #3 pearl cotton as listed in color key
- #16 tapestry needle
- #20 tapestry needle
- 1 yard ⅜-inch-wide grosgrain ribbon
- 2 (6mm) black round cabochons
- 74 (6mm) transparent faceted crystal beads #006 from The Beadery
- 9-inch x 12-inch sheet extra-thick white craft foam
- Transparent thread
- Pencil
- Hot-glue gun

Instructions
1. Cut plastic canvas according to graph. Using plastic canvas as a template, trace outline of suncatcher on craft foam, then cut ¼ inch smaller than outline.

2. Stitch and Overcast piece with #16 tapestry needle following graph, working uncoded area with royal Continental Stitches.

3. Work embroidery when background stitching and Overcasting are completed.

4. To attach beads, thread #20 tapestry needle with a 15-inch length of transparent thread. Secure thread by running needle under several stitches in back and knotting around one edge indicated at top of a cut-out hole.

5. Insert needle and thread through bead, then secure it by bringing needle around to top and down through bead again, drawing tightly to hold in place. Continue adding beads, referring to photo for number and placement.

6. When desired number of beads have been added, secure thread to corresponding bar at bottom of cut-out hole; pull tight, then run excess thread under several stitches on backside.

7. Attach remaining beads following steps 4–6. Glue craft foam to back of suncatcher.

8. For hanger, insert ribbon from back to front through small holes at top of suncatcher. Adjust to desired length and tie in a bow; trim ends as desired. ✳

COLOR KEY	
Plastic Canvas Yarn	**Yards**
■ Black #00	5
■ Red #01	3
▨ Pink #07	1
▨ Holly #27	6
☐ Sail blue #35	5
☐ White #41	41
▨ Mermaid #53	3
Uncoded area is royal #32	
Continental Stitches	18
╱ Royal #32 Overcasting	
╱ Red #01 Straight Stitch	
╱ Holly #27 Straight Stitch	
╱ Brown #15 Straight Stitch	1
╱ White #41 Backstitch and Straight Stitch	
╱ Bittersweet #52 Straight Stitch	1
○ White #41 French Knot	
#3 Pearl Cotton	
╱ Black Backstitch	1
● Attach black cabochon	
x Attach transparent thread	
Color numbers given are for Uniek Needloft plastic canvas yarn.	

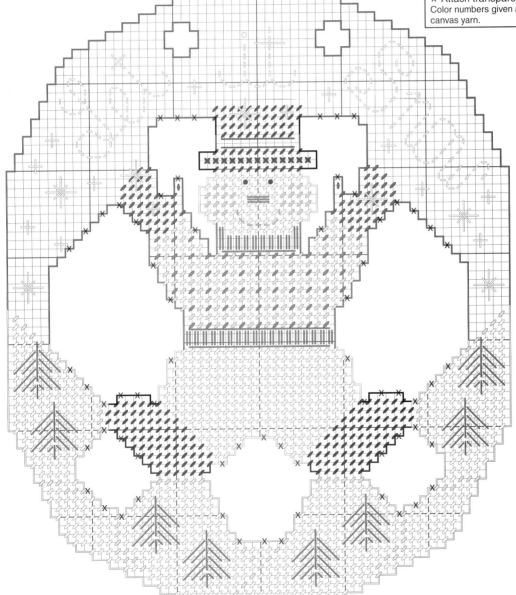

Snowman Suncatcher
60 holes x 70 holes
Cut 1

Just for Fun!

With their smiling faces and carrot noses, snowmen are favorite characters that make everyone smile! Add to your collection of lovable snowmen with these projects featuring snow friends having fun!

Wild West Snowman

Design by Janna Britton

With lasso in hand, cowboy hat on head and boots on his feet, this handsome snow-cowboy is ready to round up some fun!

Skill Level

Intermediate

Finished Size

Approximately 9 inches W x 23½ inches H, including hanger

Materials

- 1 sheet Uniek QuickCount clear 7-count plastic canvas
- ½ sheet Uniek QuickCount white 7-count plastic canvas
- Uniek Needloft plastic canvas yarn as listed in color key
- Uniek Needloft metallic craft cord as listed in color key
- DMC 6-strand embroidery floss as listed in color key
- #16 tapestry needle
- 9-inch x 14-inch piece mat board or heavy cardboard
- 9-inch x 4-inch piece mat board or heavy cardboard
- 12-inch x 12-inch sheet Snowflakes #S20026 scrapbook paper from Hot Off The Press Inc.
- 12-inch x 12-inch sheet Blue Stars #BK 05839 scrapbook paper from Sonburn
- 2 yards white rattail cord
- 3 (12-inch) lengths 22-gauge silver wire
- ¼-inch wooden dowel
- ⅛-inch hole punch
- Craft knife
- Sewing needle and white sewing thread
- Low-temperature glue gun

Cutting & Stitching

1. Cut letters from white plastic canvas; cut remaining pieces from clear plastic canvas according to graphs (this page and page 50).

2. Using craft knife through step 3, round corners on 9-inch x 14-inch piece mat board or heavy cardboard for snowman background. Set aside.

3. Using pattern given, cut sign from 9-inch x 4-inch piece mat board or heavy cardboard, but do not cut out holes at this time. Set aside.

4. Following graphs through step 8, stitch and Overcast snowman body, head, arms and cowboy hat, working uncoded areas on hat with maple Continental Stitches and uncoded areas on boot pieces with cinnamon Continental Stitches.

COLOR KEY

Plastic Canvas Yarn	Yards
☐ Pink #07	1
■ Brown #15	5
■ Royal #32	10
☐ Baby blue #36	2
☐ White #41	30
Uncoded areas on hat are maple #13 Continental Stitches	7
Uncoded areas on boots are cinnamon #14 Continental Stitches	10
⁄ Maple #13 Overcasting	
⁄ Cinnamon #14 Straight Stitch and Overcasting	
⁄ Pink #07 Straight Stitch	
○ White #41 French Knot	
Metallic Craft Cord	
■ Solid Silver #55021	4
⁄ Solid Silver #55021 Straight Stitch	
6-Strand Embroidery Floss	
⁄ Black #310 Backstitch	1
⁄ Medium navy blue #311 Backstitch and Straight Stitch	5
● Black #310 French Knot	

Color numbers given are for Uniek Needloft plastic canvas yarn and metallic craft cord and DMC 6-strand embroidery floss.

5. Work embroidery on buckle, vest, eyes and hatband. Work pink yarn Straight Stitches for mouth, working bottom stitch loosely so it loops slightly.

6. For mustache, work two slightly loose cinnamon yarn Straight Stitches from dot to dot at cheeks. Bring both strands up and work white French Knot nose over strands. Work one cinnamon Straight Stitch on each side of nose where indicated, catching mustache to hold in place for curved shape.

7. Stitch cowboy boot pieces, reversing two before stitching. Overcast top edges from dot to dot. For each boot, Whipstitch wrong sides of two pieces together along remaining unstitched edges.

8. Stitch letters, but do not Overcast edges. Work medium navy blue Backstitches when background stitching is completed.

Assembly

1. Use photo as a guide throughout assembly. Glue star paper to sign and snowflake paper to snowman background; trim excess. With hole punch, cut holes for hangers in sign

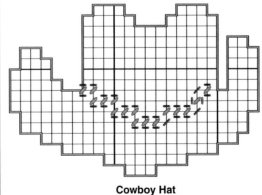

Cowboy Hat
24 holes x 16 holes
Cut 1 from clear

where indicated with white dots; cut holes at top of snowman background approximately 5¾ inches apart.

2. Glue rattail around edges of background and sign, cutting excess.

3. Wrap each length of wire around dowel to curl. Insert ends of one length through holes at top of sign, wrapping each end around wire to secure.

4. Insert ends of second length through bottom left hole on sign and through left hole on background, securing ends as for hanger at top of sign. Repeat with remaining wire on right side. Adjust curls so background hangs evenly.

5. Slip legs of snowman into boots so that toes are facing out; tack in place with cinnamon yarn. Using maple yarn, tack hat to head.

6. For rope, wrap a long length of solid silver metallic craft cord in about five circles, knotting at center top. Tie a knot in each end to prevent fraying. Tack rope to back of hand on arm A with white yarn or white sewing thread.

7. With sewing needle and white sewing thread, tack arms to body at shoulders, then tack head to neck.

8. Center and glue snowman to background. Glue letters to sign, spelling "HOWDY." ❄

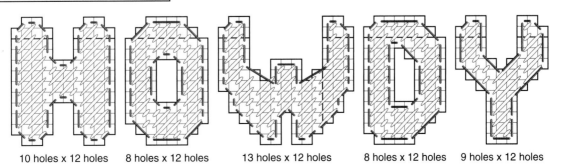

| 10 holes x 12 holes | 8 holes x 12 holes | 13 holes x 12 holes | 8 holes x 12 holes | 9 holes x 12 holes |

Sign Letters
Cut 1 each from white

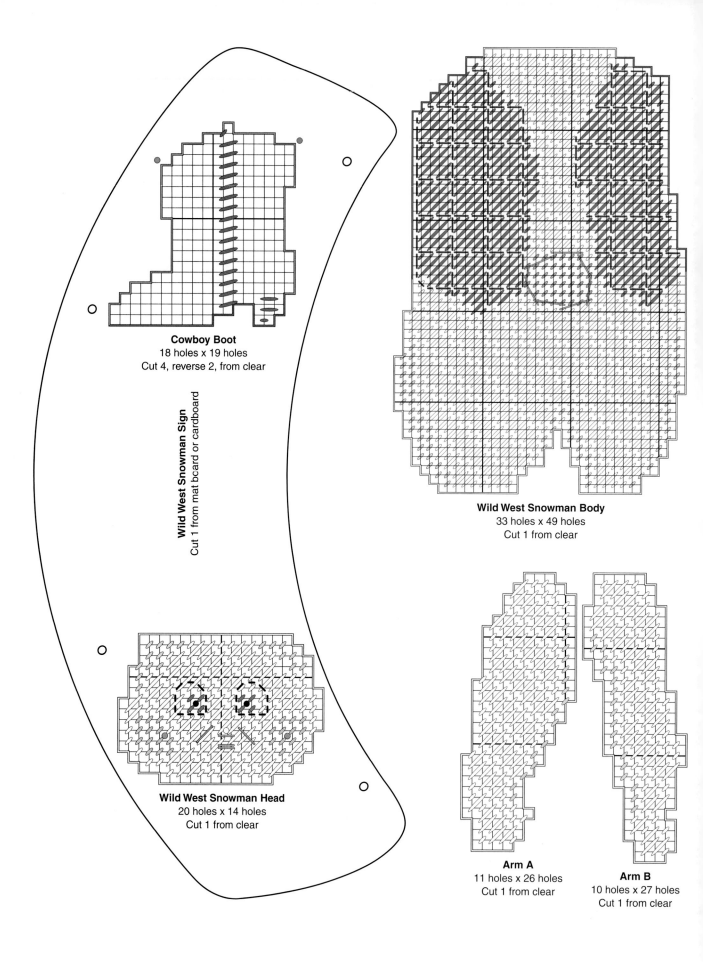

Cowboy Boot
18 holes x 19 holes
Cut 4, reverse 2, from clear

Wild West Snowman Sign
Cut 1 from mat board or cardboard

Wild West Snowman Head
20 holes x 14 holes
Cut 1 from clear

Wild West Snowman Body
33 holes x 49 holes
Cut 1 from clear

Arm A
11 holes x 26 holes
Cut 1 from clear

Arm B
10 holes x 27 holes
Cut 1 from clear

Clay Pot Snowmen

Designs by Laura Victory

Bring holiday cheer to your home with stitched snowmen and dangling miniature ornaments supported by clay pots!

Finished Size

Snowman with blue hat: 10¾ inches W x 14⅜ inches H x 2⅞ inches D

Snowman with red hat: 10 inches W x 15½ inches H x 2⅞ inches D

Snowman with green hat: 11¼ inches W x 14⅜ inches H x 2⅞ inches D

Materials

Each snowman

- ½ sheet 7-count plastic canvas
- Plastic canvas yarn as listed in color key
- #16 tapestry needle
- 2 (10mm) movable eyes
- 6mm round black bead
- 4 (4mm) round black beads
- 2-inch x 18-inch piece coordinating fabric
- 2½-inch terra cotta pot
- 12 inches ¼-inch wooden dowel
- White acrylic craft paint
- Paintbrush
- Decorative snow paint
- Pallet knife
- Sandpaper
- Plaster of paris
- Sewing needle and white sewing thread
- Hot-glue gun

Snowman With Blue Hat

- ⅞-inch white button
- 4 miniature dimensional snowflake ornaments
- Light blue acrylic craft paint
- Thin silver cord

Snowman With Red Hat

- ¾-inch white button
- 2 red buttons in differing sizes
- 2 green buttons in differing sizes
- Red acrylic craft paint

Snowman With Green Hat

- Uniek Needloft metallic craft cord as listed in color key
- 4 miniature red and green plastic candy ornaments
- Dark green acrylic craft paint
- Clear nylon monofilament

Skill Level

Beginner

Cutting & Stitching

1. Cut plastic canvas according to graphs.

2. Stitch and Overcast pieces following graphs, working uncoded areas with white Continental Stitches and reversing one arm for each snowman before stitching.

Base Preparation

1. Sand terra cotta pots; brush off residue.

2. Mix plaster of paris and fill pots. Insert wooden dowel about 2 inches into wet mix through hole in bottom of pot. *Note: Mix should be thick enough so it won't leak through hole in bottom of pot and so it will hold dowel in place.* Allow to dry thoroughly.

3. Paint dowel white and pot with corresponding color. Allow to dry, then paint a second coat; allow to dry.

4. Using pallet knife, dab pot with decorative snow paint around dowel and as desired around pot.

Assembly

1. Use photo as a guide throughout assembly. Using tapestry needle and white yarn, attach arms to backside of snowmen at shoulder areas.

2. Glue movable eyes to head where indicated on graphs. Using sewing needle and white sewing thread, attach 6mm beads to heads for noses and 4mm beads to heads for mouths where indicated on graphs. Using sewing needle and white thread, attach ¾-inch white button to red hat.

3. Tie fabric around necks for scarves; glue to secure. For snowman with blue hat, glue ⅞-inch white button to scarf on knot.

4. Using silver cord, attach snowflake ornaments to arms of snowman with

blue hat at red dots, allowing 1½ inches between snowflakes and arms.

5. Using varying lengths of white thread, attach buttons to arms of snowman with red hat at red dots.

6. Using clear nylon monofilament, attach candy ornaments to arms of snowman with green hat at red dots, allowing 2½ inches between candy and arms.

7. Attach snowmen to corresponding dowels with tapestry needle and white yarn, stitching through yarn on backside of snowmen. ✳

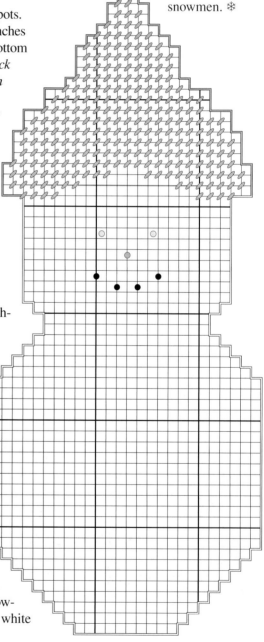

Snowman With Blue Hat
26 holes x 60 holes
Cut 1

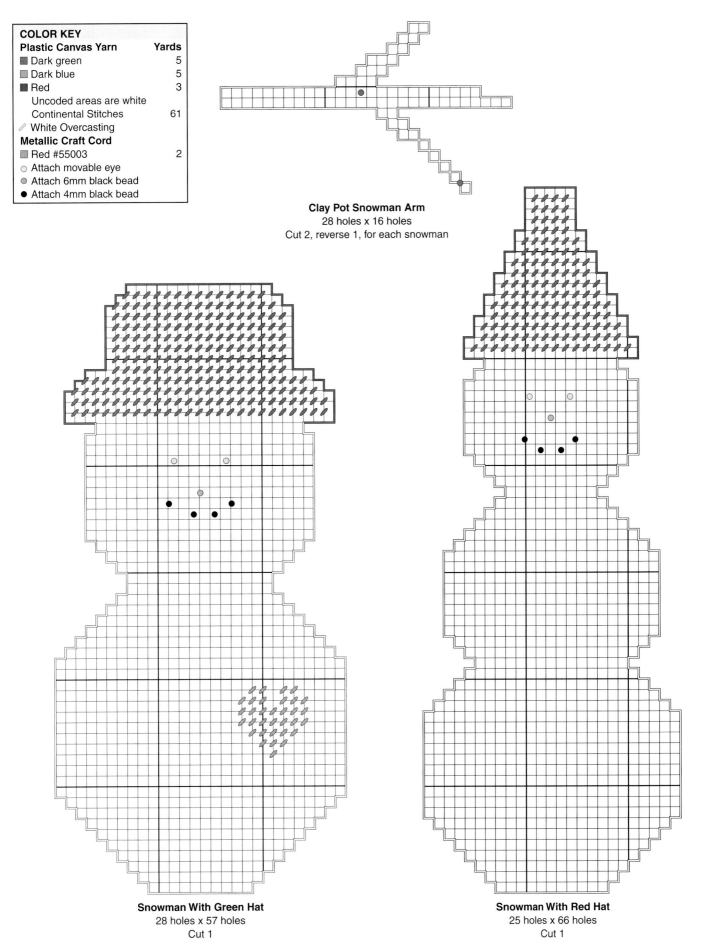

COLOR KEY

Plastic Canvas Yarn	Yards
■ Dark green	5
■ Dark blue	5
■ Red	3
Uncoded areas are white	
Continental Stitches	61
⁄ White Overcasting	
Metallic Craft Cord	
■ Red #55003	2
○ Attach movable eye	
● Attach 6mm black bead	
● Attach 4mm black bead	

Clay Pot Snowman Arm
28 holes x 16 holes
Cut 2, reverse 1, for each snowman

Snowman With Green Hat
28 holes x 57 holes
Cut 1

Snowman With Red Hat
25 holes x 66 holes
Cut 1

Eskimo Shadow Box

Design by Lee Lindeman

apture the vibrant beauty of an Alaskan sunset with this one-of-a-kind shadow-box project!

Skill Level
Intermediate

Finished Size
8⅛ inches W x 8¾ inches H x 2¾ inches D

Materials
- 2 sheets 7-count plastic canvas
- Worsted weight yarn as listed in color key
- 6-strand embroidery floss as listed in color key
- #16 tapestry needle
- 8¼-inch square shadow box
- FolkArt licorice #938 acrylic craft paint from Plaid Enterprises Inc.
- Paintbrush
- FolkArt Clearcote Hi-Shine Glaze high-gloss spray finish from Plaid Enterprises Inc.
- Sheet beige felt
- Craft foam or thin plastic foam
- Tacky glue
- Hot-glue gun

Cutting, Stitching & Painting

1. Paint shadow box with licorice paint; allow to dry thoroughly. Spray with high-gloss finish; allow to dry.

2. Cut plastic canvas according to graphs (pages 55 and 57). Cut felt slightly smaller than Eskimo and lower legs.

3. Stitch base pieces following graph, reversing base bottom before stitching. Work Backstitches with black floss on base top only. Whipstitch wrong sides together with white.

4. Stitch and Overcast remaining pieces following graphs, working Continental Stitches in uncoded areas on pieces as follows: Eskimo face with pale pink; Eskimo coat, upper legs and lower legs with light taupe; background behind sunset with light yellow.

5. Work black floss Backstitches and French Knots when background stitching and Overcasting are completed.

Assembly

1. Use photo as a guide throughout assembly. Using tacky glue through step 3, glue felt to back of Eskimo and lower legs.

2. Glue background inside box to back wall, making sure top edge is

flush against ceiling of box. With back edge flush against background, glue base to floor of box.

3. For separators, glue a few small squares or rectangles of craft foam or plastic foam to back of each iceberg and to back of Eskimo along bottom edge.

4. Using glue gun through step 5, glue back iceberg to base with separators touching background. Next glue front iceberg to base with separators touching back iceberg. Glue igloo to base on right side and to front iceberg.

5. Glue body to base toward front on left side allowing just enough room for upper legs. Glue upper legs to base along bottom edge of body, then glue lower legs to front edges of upper legs.

6. Hang as desired. ✷

COLOR KEY	
Worsted Weight Yarn	**Yards**
☐ White	30
■ Purple	9
■ Bright pink	5
☐ Ecru	4
■ Orange	4
☐ Bright yellow	3
■ Medium blue	1
☐ Light gray	1
■ Red	1
■ Black	1
Uncoded areas on background are light yellow Continental Stitches	7
Uncoded areas on Eskimo coat and legs are light taupe Continental Stitches	5
Uncoded area on face is pale pink Continental Stitches	1
⁄ Light yellow Overcasting	
⁄ Light taupe Overcasting	
6-Strand Embroidery Floss	
⁄ Black Backstitch	9
● Black French Knot	

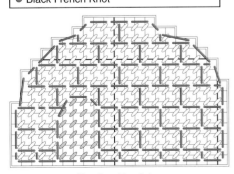

Shadow Box Igloo
21 holes x 14 holes
Cut 1

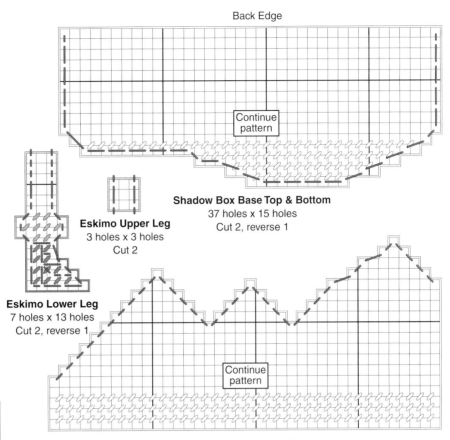

Back Edge

Continue pattern

Shadow Box Base Top & Bottom
37 holes x 15 holes
Cut 2, reverse 1

Eskimo Upper Leg
3 holes x 3 holes
Cut 2

Eskimo Lower Leg
7 holes x 13 holes
Cut 2, reverse 1

Continue pattern

Shadow Box Front Iceberg
38 holes x 18 holes
Cut 1

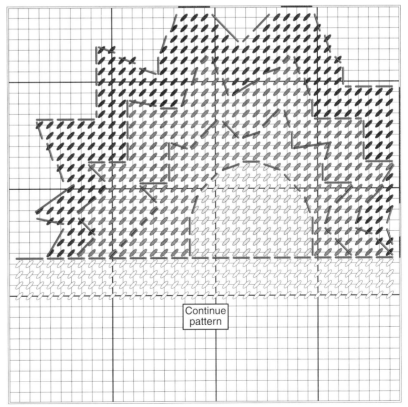

Continue pattern

Shadow Box Background
38 holes x 37 holes
Cut 1

Graphs continued on page 57

Snowman Pillow Appliqué

Design by Joan Green

Dress up an ordinary pillow with this frosty friend! A variety of stitches accented with glistening French Knots makes this a fun project to stitch!

Skill Level
Beginner

Finished Size
Appliqué only: 6⅞ inches W x 8 inches H

Materials
- ½ sheet 7-count plastic canvas
- Coats & Clark Red Heart Classic worsted weight yarn Art. E267 as listed in color key
- Coats & Clark Red Heart Super Saver worsted weight yarn Art. E300 as listed in color key
- ¹⁄₁₆-inch-wide Plastic Canvas 10 Metallic Needlepoint Yarn by Rainbow Gallery as listed in color key
- Arctic Rays Wispy Fringe by Rainbow Gallery as listed in color key
- #16 tapestry needle
- Purchased throw pillow
- Repositionable glue
- White craft glue

Instructions

1. Cut plastic canvas according to graphs.

2. Stitch and Overcast pieces following graphs. When background stitching is completed, work silver snowflakes on scarf and green Straight Stitches on leaves. Using a double strand of wispy fringe, work French Knots on face.

3. Using photo as a guide, attach nose to face and holly sprig to hat with craft glue.

4. Spread a liberal amount of repositionable glue to wrong side of stitched piece and allow to air dry overnight. *Note: Glue will remain tacky.* Attach to center of pillow. ❄

COLOR KEY	
Worsted Weight Yarn	**Yards**
☐ White #1	8
■ Black #310	1
■ Medium coral #252	1
■ Grass green #687	1
■ Light raspberry #774	1
■ Olympic blue #849	10
☐ Blue #886	12
■ Cherry red #912	1
╱ Grass green #687 Straight Stitch	
╱ Olympic blue #849 Backstitch	
¹/₁₆-Inch Metallic Needlepoint Yarn	
╱ Silver #PM52 Straight Stitch	2
● Silver #PM52 French Knot	
Wispy Fringe	
● White #AR2 French Knot	5

Color numbers given are for Coats & Clark Red Heart Classic worsted weight yarn Art. E267 and Super Saver worsted weight yarn Art. E300, and Rainbow Gallery Plastic Canvas 10 Metallic Needlepoint Yarn and Arctic Rays Wispy Fringe.

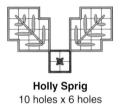

Holly Sprig
10 holes x 6 holes
Cut 1

Carrot Nose
7 holes x 4 holes
Cut 1

Snowman Appliqué
45 holes x 54 holes
Cut 1

Eskimo Shadow Box

Continued from page 55

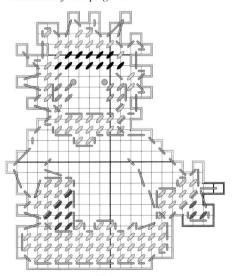

Eskimo
21 holes x 24 holes
Cut 1

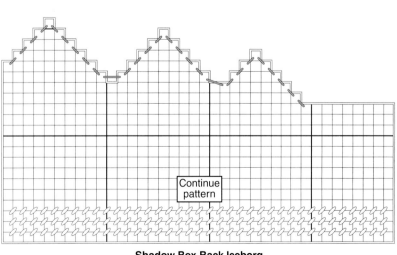

Shadow Box Back Iceberg
38 holes x 21 holes
Cut 1

Continue pattern

Caroling Penguin

Design by Judy Collishaw

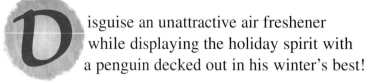

Disguise an unattractive air freshener while displaying the holiday spirit with a penguin decked out in his winter's best!

COLOR KEY

Worsted Weight Yarn	Yards
■ Black	34
□ White	9
▨ Yellow	5
■ Red	4
■ Paddy green	2
Uncoded areas are black Continental Stitches	
⁄ Black Straight Stitch	
#5 Pearl Cotton	
⁄ Black #310 Backstitch and Straight Stitch	1
#3 Pearl Cotton	
⁄ Medium rose #899 Straight Stitch	1
Color numbers given are for DMC pearl cotton.	

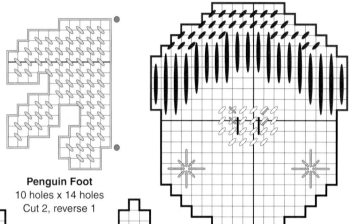

Penguin Foot
10 holes x 14 holes
Cut 2, reverse 1

Penguin Head
19 holes x 21 holes
Cut 1

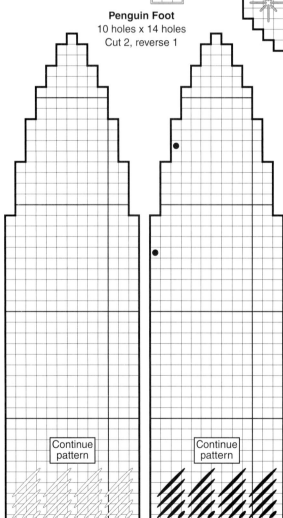

Penguin Wing
20 holes x 15 holes
Cut 2, reverse 1

Songbook
11 holes x 15 holes
Cut 2

Penguin Body Front
13 holes x 46 holes
Cut 1

Penguin Body Side & Back
13 holes x 46 holes
Cut 4

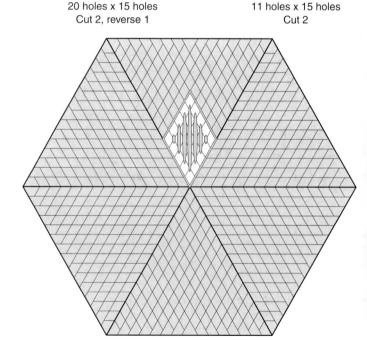

Penguin Beak
Cut 1 from hexagon,
cutting away gray area

Continue pattern

Continue pattern

Skill Level

Beginner

Finished Size

5⅛ inches W x 8½ inches H x 4⅝ inches D

Materials

- 1 sheet 7-count plastic canvas
- 5-inch Uniek QuickShape plastic canvas hexagon
- Worsted weight yarn as listed in color key
- DMC #3 pearl cotton as listed in color key
- DMC #5 pearl cotton as listed in color key
- #16 tapestry needle
- ½-inch green pompom
- 1¼-inch x 20-inch piece plaid flannel
- Low-temperature glue gun

Instructions

1. Cut plastic canvas according to graphs, cutting away gray area on plastic canvas hexagon.

2. Stitch pieces following graphs, working uncoded areas with black Continental Stitches and reversing one wing and one foot before stitching.

3. When background stitching is completed, work black yarn Straight Stitches for eyes; work pearl cotton embroidery on face and songbook.

4. Following graphs throughout, Overcast head, beak and wings. With wrong sides facing, Whipstitch song-book pieces together along one long edge, then Overcast remaining edges.

5. Use photo as a guide through step 8. With black, Whipstitch body pieces together, easing as necessary to fit and making sure to stitch over top point of body with yarn. *Note: There will be two back pieces, two side pieces and one front piece.*

6. Overcast bottom edges of body front and back pieces with adjacent colors. Using yellow throughout, Overcast feet. With right sides

together, Whipstitch straight edges of feet from blue dot to blue dot to bottom edges of body sides over previous Overcasting.

7. Glue as follows: head to body front, with eyes at top of body; top part of beak to head below eyes; pompom to

top of hat; wings to body sides, placing back edge of wings between red dots at edges adjacent to body back; front edges of songbook to front seams so that wings appear to hold book.

8. For scarf, wrap plaid flannel around neck, tying at side. ❋

Snow Girl Dress-Up Doll

Designs by Janna Britton

Children will love dressing up their very own snow dolls! Stitch an entire wardrobe as shown, or in colors to match some of your child's outfits!

Skill Level

Intermediate

Finished Size

Snow girl: 3 inches W x 6 inches H

Dress: 3¾ inches W x 4¾ inches H

Overalls: 3⅜ inches W x 4¼ inches H

Skirt: 3⅛ inches W x 2¾ inches H

Vest: 2⅜ inches W x 3 inches H

Coat: 3⅜ inches W x 4 inches H

Top hat: 2⅛ inches W x 2 inches H

Knit hat: 2¼ inches W x 1½ inches H, including pompom

Blond wig: 2 inches W x 1⅞ inches H

Pigtail wig: 3¾ inches W x 2 inches H, including pigtails

Materials

- 1 sheet Uniek QuickCount clear 7-count plastic canvas
- ½ sheet Uniek QuickCount white 7-count plastic canvas
- Uniek Needloft plastic canvas yarn as listed in color key
- DMC #3 pearl cotton as listed in color key
- DMC 6-strand embroidery floss as listed in color key
- #16 tapestry needle
- 7 inches ⅜-inch-wide white hook-and-loop tape
- ½-inch yellow pompom
- Sewing needle and sewing thread
- Low-temperature glue gun

Snow Girl & Clothing

1. Cut snow girl front and back from white plastic canvas according to graph (page 63). Snow girl back will remain unstitched.

2. Stitch front following graph. When background stitching is completed, use 1 ply brown yarn to work Backstitches around eyes and French Knots for mouth. Use full strand pumpkin yarn to work French Knot nose. Backstitch arm details with dark steel gray pearl cotton.

3. Stitch soft side of hook-and-loop tape to front where indicated on graph with blue hearts. Whipstitch front and unstitched back together with white.

4. Cut dress, overalls, skirt, vest and coat from clear plastic canvas according to graphs (pages 62 and 63).

5. Stitch and Overcast pieces following graphs, working uncoded areas on dress with pink Continental Stitches, uncoded areas on overalls with sail blue Continental Stitches and uncoded areas on skirt and vest with dark royal Continental Stitches.

6. Work embroidery on vest with black floss and full strand red yarn. Work embroidery on dress with medium navy blue floss and on overalls, skirt and coat with black floss.

7. Work ½-inch-long yellow Turkey Loop Stitches where indicated on coat. Cut loops; fray slightly to resemble fringe.

Hats & Wigs

1. Cut pieces for top hat, knit hat, blond wig and pigtail wig from clear plastic canvas according to graphs (pages 62 and 63).

2. Stitch hat and wig pieces following graphs, overlapping Slanted Gobelin Stitches at center top of blond wig front.

3. Overcast bottom edges of hat and wig pieces from dot to dot. For bangs on blond wig, bring ends of two or three lengths of yarn down under stitches at center top of front so center fold is hooked over a stitch at top. Allow lengths to extend ¼ inch past edge as in photo.

4. Whipstitch wrong sides of corresponding hat and wig pieces together along remaining unstitched edges.

5. Work yellow Straight Stitches on knit hat.

6. Using photo as a guide through step 7, on both front and back pieces of pigtail wig, thread one to two lengths of yarn under each Continental Stitch on center vertical bar (at arrow), allowing 1 inch to extend past each side edge of head.

7. Gather yarn together in a pigtail on each side and tie with another length of maple yarn; secure with a knot and clip ends to same length as pigtails.

Finishing

1. Cut a 1-inch length each of rough side of hook-and-loop tape for dress, overalls, skirt, vest and coat.

2. Lay tape over smooth side of hook-and-loop tape already on body, then apply glue to back of tape. Place one clothing piece over snow girl, then press piece on glued area of hook-and-loop tape. When glue is cooled, remove clothing piece.

3. Repeat with remaining clothing pieces. *Note: Hat and wigs fit over head so hook-and-loop tape is not needed.* ❋

COLOR KEY

Plastic Canvas Yarn	Yards
■ Red #01	18
□ Maple #13	10
■ Brown #15	1
■ Royal #32	2
■ Baby blue #36	1
□ White #41	15
■ Dark royal #48	11
□ Yellow #57	9
Uncoded areas on dress are pink #07 Continental Stitches	13
Uncoded areas on overalls are sail blue #35 Continental Stitches	10
Uncoded areas on vest and skirt are dark royal #48 Continental Stitches	
⁄ Pink #07 Overcasting	
⁄ Sail blue #35 Overcasting	
⁄ Red #01 Straight Stitch	
⁄ Brown #15 Backstitch	
⁄ Yellow #57 Straight Stitch	
● Red #01 French Knot	
● Pumpkin #12 French Knot	1
● Brown #15 French Knot	
○ Yellow #57 Turkey Loop Stitch	1
#3 Pearl Cotton	
⁄ Dark steel gray #415 Backstitch	5
6-Strand Embroidery Floss	
⁄ Black #310 Backstitch	2
⁄ Medium navy blue #311 Backstitch and Straight Stitch	
● Black #310 French Knot	

Color numbers given are for Uniek Needloft plastic canvas yarn and DMC #3 pearl cotton and 6-strand embroidery floss.

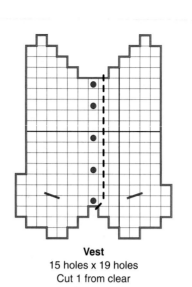

Vest
15 holes x 19 holes
Cut 1 from clear

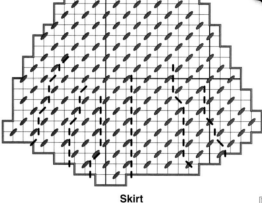

Skirt
25 holes x 18 holes
Cut 1 from clear

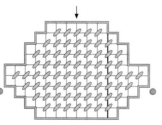

Pigtail Wig Back
14 holes x 9 holes
Cut 1 from clear

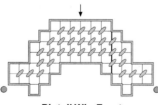

Pigtail Wig Front
14 holes x 7 holes
Cut 1 from clear

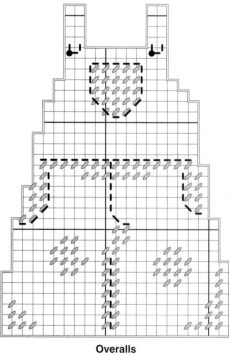

Overalls
22 holes x 31 holes
Cut 1 from clear

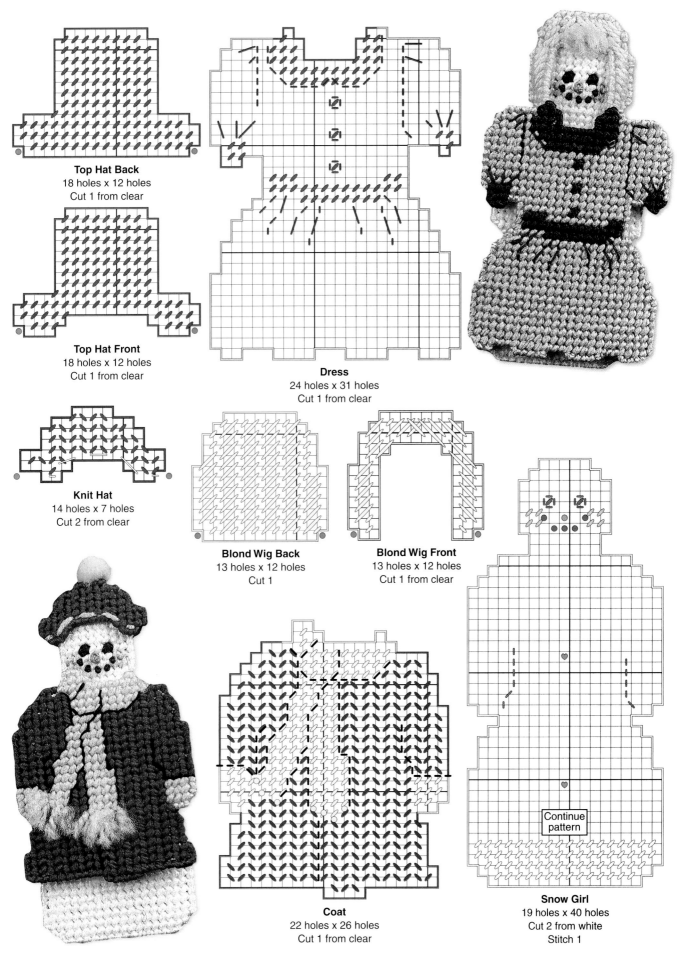

Top Hat Back
18 holes x 12 holes
Cut 1 from clear

Top Hat Front
18 holes x 12 holes
Cut 1 from clear

Knit Hat
14 holes x 7 holes
Cut 2 from clear

Dress
24 holes x 31 holes
Cut 1 from clear

Blond Wig Back
13 holes x 12 holes
Cut 1

Blond Wig Front
13 holes x 12 holes
Cut 1 from clear

Continue
pattern

Coat
22 holes x 26 holes
Cut 1 from clear

Snow Girl
19 holes x 40 holes
Cut 2 from white
Stitch 1

Peppermint Snowman Advent Calendar

Design by Joan Green

Counting down the days until Christmas is as fun as can be with this delightful skinny snowman advent calendar!

Skill Level

Beginner

Finished Size

5¾ inches W x 20½ inches H

Materials

- 1 artist-size sheet 7-count plastic canvas
- Coats & Clark Red Heart Classic worsted weight yarn Art. E267 as listed in color key
- Coats & Clark Red Heart Super Saver worsted weight yarn Art. E300 as listed in color key
- #16 tapestry needle
- ¾-inch gold jingle bell
- 5¾ yards ⅛-inch-wide red satin ribbon
- 25 round wrapped peppermint candies
- Sawtooth hanger
- Fabric glue

Instructions

1. Cut snowman from plastic canvas according to graphs (page 66). *Note: Cut and stitch plastic canvas as one piece, not two separate pieces.*

2. Cut red satin ribbon in 25 (8-inch) lengths. Set aside.

3. Stitch and Overcast piece following graphs, working uncoded area on head with white Continental Stitches and continuing Slanted Gobelin and Continental Stitch pattern on body as shown.

4. When background stitching is completed, use full strand yarn to work red Straight Stitches for stripes on scarf, black Backstitches for mouth and eyebrows and white French Knots on body, wrapping yarn two times around needle.

5. Using 2 plies yarn throughout, work white French Knots on cap band and mittens, wrapping yarn around needle one time; work snowflakes on scarf, placing a French Knot at ends of stitches and one in center of each snowflake. Backstitch arm and scarf details with black.

6. Using photo as a guide through step 7, thread one length of red ribbon through hanger on jingle bell, then thread ribbon ends through yarn on backside at tip of stocking cap, allowing bell to hang freely. Knot ends to secure.

7. One by one, thread ends of remaining lengths of ribbon from back to front through each set of holes indicated for attaching peppermint candy. Beginning at bottom, tie a wrapped candy to snowman with each ribbon.

8. Center and glue sawtooth hanger to top backside of cap with fabric glue. ❈

COLOR KEY	
Worsted Weight Yarn	**Yards**
☐ White #1	56
■ Black #310	2
▦ Pink #737	1
▨ Delft blue #885	2
▢ Blue #886	10
■ Cherry red #912	6
Uncoded area on head is white #1 Continental Stitches	
⁄ White #1 (2-ply) Straight Stitch	
⁄ Black #310 Backstitch	
⁄ Cherry red #912 Straight Stitch	
○ White #1 (2-ply) French Knot	
● White #1 (4-ply) French Knot	
● Attach peppermint candy	
Color numbers given are for Coats & Clark Red Heart Classic worsted weight yarn Art. E267 and Super Saver worsted weight yarn Art. E300.	

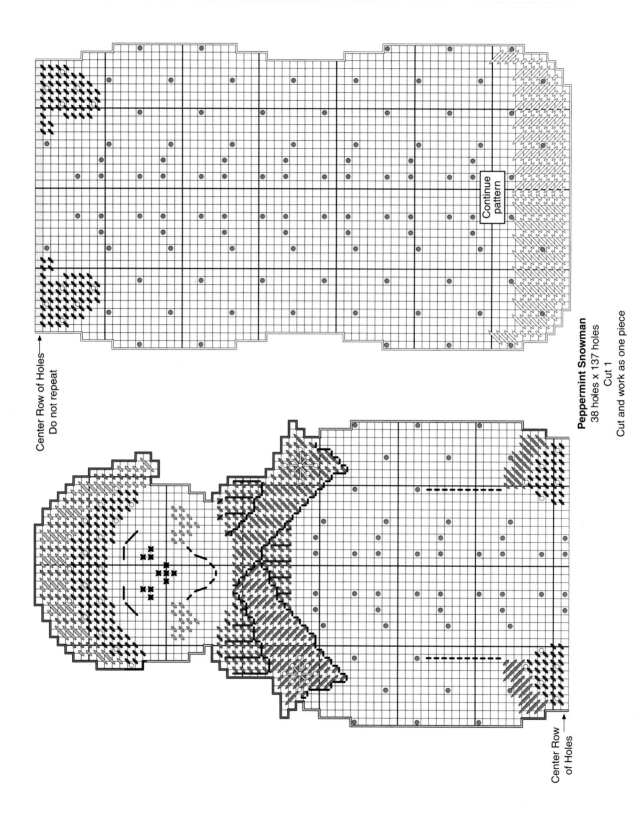

Center Row of Holes →
Do not repeat

Continue pattern

Peppermint Snowman
38 holes x 137 holes
Cut 1
Cut and work as one piece

Center Row
of Holes →

Silly Snowman Ornament

Design by Valerie Leinberger

This special ornament was designed just for kids, by a kid! Hang this friendly snowman in a window and watch him twirl in a breeze!

Skill Level

Beginner

Finished Size

2⅞ inches W x 5¾ inches H, excluding hanger

Materials

- ½ sheet 7-count plastic canvas
- Uniek Needloft plastic canvas yarn as listed in color key
- #16 tapestry needle

Instructions

1. Cut plastic canvas according to graphs.

2. Stitch pieces following graphs, working uncoded areas with white Continental Stitches.

3. When background stitching is completed, using a full strand of yarn throughout, work pumpkin French Knot for nose, wrapping yarn around needle three times and royal French Knots for buttons, wrapping yarn around needle one time. Work royal Backstitches for hatband on hat.

4. Using 1 ply yarn throughout, work black Backstitches for mouth and fern Backstitches for holly leaves. Work black French Knots for eyes and red French Knot for holly berry, wrapping yarn around needle for each French Knot one time.

5. For ornament hanger, cut desired length black yarn and fasten ends to center top backside of one hat piece.

6. Cut about a 1-inch length black yarn; glue ends to center bottom backside of one hat piece and center top backside one head piece.

7. Cut a 3-inch length white yarn. Glue one end to center bottom backside of one head piece and other end to center top backside of one bottom piece. Center and glue one middle piece to yarn between head and bottom pieces.

8. Whipstitch wrong sides of corresponding pieces together following graphs. ✳

COLOR KEY	
Plastic Canvas Yarn	**Yards**
■ Black #00	2
▨ Brown#15	1
Uncoded areas are white #41 Continental Stitches	7
⁄ White #41 Whipstitching	
⁄ Black #00 Backstitch	
⁄ Fern #23 Backstitch	1
⁄ Royal #32 Backstitch	1
● Black #00 French Knot	
● Red #01 French Knot	1
● Pumpkin #12 French Knot	1
● Royal #32 French Knot	
Color numbers given are for Uniek Needloft plastic canvas yarn.	

Silly Snowman Hat
7 holes x 4 holes
Cut 2

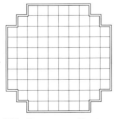

Silly Snowman Bottom
10 holes x 10 holes
Cut 2

Silly Snowman Head
7 holes x 7 holes
Cut 2

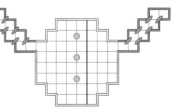

Silly Snowman Middle
18 holes x 9 holes
Cut 2

Smiling Snowman Purse

Design by Susan Leinberger

Little ones can tuck all sorts of goodies into this kid-size purse! Fill it on Christmas morning as an alternative to a stocking!

COLOR KEY

Plastic Canvas Yarn	Yards
■ Black #00	25
▫ Pink #07	2
▪ Sail blue #35	5
▫ White #41	45
▪ Bittersweet #52	1
▪ Watermelon #55	1

Uncoded areas are white #41
Continental Stitches
✏ Watermelon #55 Backstitches
and Straight Stitches

Metallic Craft Cord

▪ White/silver #55008	4

#3 Pearl Cotton

✏ Black Backstitch and Straight Stitch	1

● Attach nose

Color numbers given are for Uniek Needloft plastic canvas yarn and metallic craft cord.

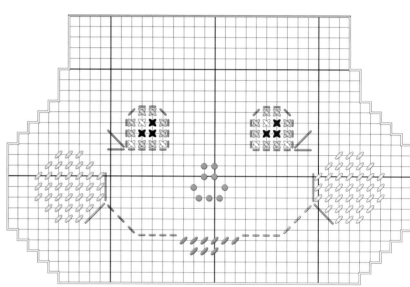

Purse Front & Back
39 holes x 25 holes
Cut 2
Stitch front as graphed,
Stitch back entirely with white
Continental Stitches

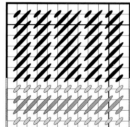

Hat Side
12 holes x 12 holes
Cut 2

Purse Nose
3 holes x 4 holes
Cut 3

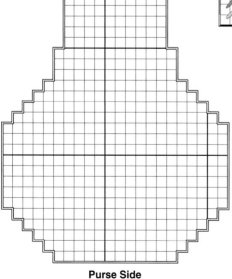

Purse Side
22 holes x 25 holes
Cut 2

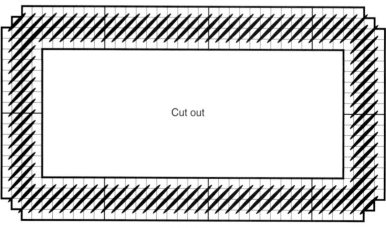

Cut out

Hat Brim
37 holes x 20 holes
Cut 2

Skill Level

Beginner

Finished Size

5⅝ inches W x 5½ inches H x 3⅜ inches D

Materials

- 2 sheets Uniek QuickCount 7-count plastic canvas
- Uniek Needloft plastic canvas yarn as listed in color key
- Uniek Needloft metallic craft cord as listed in color key
- #3 pearl cotton as listed in color key
- #16 tapestry needle
- 1 yard ¼-inch white-silver twisted cord
- Hot-glue gun

Purse

1. Cut nose pieces and purse front, back and sides from plastic canvas according to graphs.

2. Cut one 29-hole x 12-hole piece for purse bottom and stitch with white Continental Stitches.

3. Following graphs through step 6, stitch nose pieces. Whipstitch together around sides and tip, making sure to cover tip completely.

4. Stitch purse front and sides, working uncoded areas with white Continental Stitches. Stitch back entirely with white Continental Stitches.

5. Work embroidery for eyes with black pearl cotton and for mouth with watermelon yarn. Whipstitch unstitched edges of nose to front where indicated on graph.

6. Using white, Whipstitch front and back to sides, then Whipstitch front, back and sides to bottom. Overcast top edges with silver.

Hat

1. Cut hat pieces from plastic canvas according to graphs.

2. Stitch pieces following graphs. Overcast inside edges of hat top with black.

3. Using adjacent colors through step 4, Whipstitch front and back to sides, then Whipstitch front, back and sides to top.

4. Whipstitch wrong sides of hat brim pieces together along outside edges. Whipstitch bottom edges of hat front, back and sides to inside edges of hat brim through all three thicknesses.

Final Assembly

1. Thread ends of white/silver twisted cord through holes on hat top to inside; pull completely through.

2. Glue ends of cord to wrong side of purse sides from bottom to top edge. When glue has set, pull hat down over top of purse. ✲

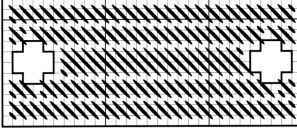

Hat Top
29 holes x 12 holes
Cut 1

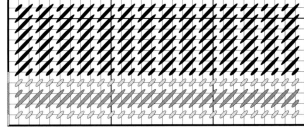

Hat Front & Back
29 holes x 12 holes
Cut 2

Layered Snowflake Frame

Design by Kathy Wirth

ow many layers does a snowflake have? This one has six, with enough room to display a favorite picture!

Skill Level

Intermediate

Finished Size

5½ inches W x 5¾ inches H, excluding hanger

Materials

- 6 (5-inch) Uniek QuickShape plastic canvas hexagons
- ⅛-inch-wide Plastic Canvas 7 Metallic Needlepoint Yarn from Rainbow Gallery as listed in color key
- #16 tapestry needle
- 18 inches ⅝-inch-wide sheer white ribbon
- Photo
- Hot-glue gun

Instructions

1. Cut plastic canvas according to graphs, cutting away gray areas from hexagons.

2. Matching edges, hold each pair of layers together and stitch through both thicknesses. Apply glue to back of stitched areas as necessary to secure yarn ends. Edges will remain unstitched.

3. With right sides facing up, glue layer B on top of layer A, so that spokes of layer B are placed evenly between spokes of layer A.

4. Trim photo to 2¼-inch circle. Glue to center of assembly, making sure top of photo is aligned with a spoke of snowflake B. Glue layer C over photo, matching edges of points with layer B.

5. For hanger, attach desired length of metallic needlepoint yarn to top spoke of snowflake; secure with glue.

6. Tie sheer white ribbon in a bow around base of hanger; trim ends. ❊

Layer A
Cut 2
Cut away gray areas

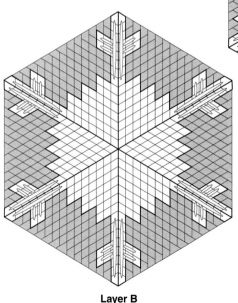

Layer B
Cut 2
Cut away gray areas

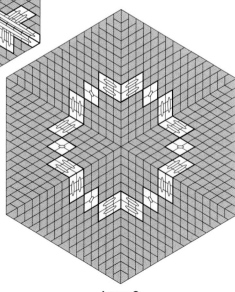

Layer C
Cut 2
Cut away gray areas

COLOR KEY	
⅛-Inch Metallic Yarn	Yards
☐ White pearl #PC10	5
Color numbers given are for Rainbow Gallery Plastic Canvas 7 Metallic Needlepoint Yarn.	

Jeweled Snowflake
Instructions begin on next page.

Jeweled Snowflake

Design by Joan Green

ttach this snowflake motif to a dark pillow for a stunning accent. Make several and glue others to gift boxes or album covers, or hang as large tree ornaments! See photo on page 71.

Skill Level

Intermediate

Finished Size

Appliqué only: 7⅛ inches W x 7⅛ inches H

Materials

- ½ sheet 7-count plastic canvas
- Faux Fur very furry singles yarn by Rainbow Gallery as listed in color key
- Arctic Rays Wispy Fringe by Rainbow Gallery as listed in color key
- #16 tapestry needle
- 4 (8mm) crystal #006 round acrylic faceted stones by The Beadery from Designs by Joan Green
- 8 (9mm) antique white pearl #427 round acrylic cabochons by The Beadery from Designs by Joan Green
- 16mm antique white pearl #427 round acrylic cabochon by The Beadery from Designs by Joan Green
- Dark-colored purchased throw pillow
- Jewel glue
- Fabric glue

Instructions

1. Cut plastic canvas according to graph, cutting away gray areas.

2. Cut furry yarn and wispy fringe in 1 yard lengths, then combining one length of each, Overcast snowflake

following graph, working Continental Stitches while Overcasting.

3. Using jewel glue, attach faceted stones and cabochons to snowflake where indicated on graph.

4. Using fabric glue, attach snowflake to pillow. ❄

COLOR KEY	
Furry Yarn and Wispy Fringe	**Yards**
☐ Ermine (white) #FF1 and white #AR2	15 each
● Attach 8mm crystal stone	
○ Attach 9mm antique white pearl cabochon	
○ Attach 16mm antique white pearl cabochon	
Color numbers given are for Rainbow Gallery Faux Fur very furry singles yarn and Arctic Rays Wispy Fringe.	

Jeweled Snowflake
47 holes x 47 holes
Cut 1,
cutting away gray areas

Penguin Pals

Design by Lee Lindeman

 dd a fun, wintry touch to your dining table with this delightful centerpiece! A father penguin and his baby penguin are collecting snowballs at the North Pole!

Skill Level

Intermediate

Materials

- 2 sheets 7-count plastic canvas
- Coats & Clark Red Heart Super Saver worsted weight yarn Art. E300 as listed in color key
- #16 tapestry needle
- 2 (4mm) black beads
- 2 black seed beads
- 2 (6mm) black cabochons
- 3 (5⁄16-inch) heart buttons
- ¾-inch red bow tie button or 6 inches ¼-inch-wide red satin ribbon
- 9½-inch x 12½-inch piece blue felt
- 7-inch x 9-inch piece white felt
- Small amount black craft foam
- 9-inch x 12-inch solid wood oval plaque from Walnut Hollow
- Acrylic craft paint in medium blue and light blue
- FolkArt Clearcote Hi-Shine Glaze high-gloss spray finish from Plaid Enterprises Inc.
- Paintbrush
- 1 pair small yellow toddler socks
- 3 inches 19-gauge wire
- Hand drill and bit to fit 19-gauge wire
- Small amount plastic foam
- Small amount fiberfill
- Sewing needle
- Yellow and black sewing thread
- Tacky glue
- Hot-glue gun

Finished Size

12½ inches W x 9⅞ inches H x 9½ inches D

Cutting & Stitching

1. Cut plastic canvas according to graphs (pages 74 and 75). Cut penguin beak pieces from black craft foam following patterns given (pages 74 and 75). Cut white felt slightly smaller than floating iceberg. Cut blue felt to fit bottom of oval plaque.

2. Work all uncoded areas on all penguin pieces with black Continental Stitches. Following graphs through step 6, stitch floating iceberg, upright iceberg bottom, feet pieces and father's head pieces. Overcast floating iceberg with white.

3. Stitch baby head front as graphed. Stitch baby head back entirely with black Continental Stitches.

4. Stitch father and baby body fronts as graphed, Overcasting top edges with white and black. Stitch body backs entirely with black Continental Stitches, Overcasting top edges with black.

5. For each penguin, stitch two arms as graphed; reverse two and stitch with black Reverse Continental Stitches.

6. Stitch upright iceberg and fish pieces as graphed, reversing one of each before stitching.

Assembly

1. Use photo as a guide throughout assembly. Whipstitch corresponding body fronts and backs together along side edges, then Whipstitch bottom pieces to bottom edges. Stuff bodies with fiberfill through neck opening.

2. Using sewing needle and black thread, attach 4mm black beads to father's face where indicated on graph; attach seed beads to baby's face where indicated on graph.

3. Whipstitch corresponding head pieces together, stuffing with fiberfill before closing. Insert and hot glue heads into bodies at neck openings.

4. For each arm, Whipstitch wrong sides of two corresponding arm pieces together. Hot glue arms to shoulders, making sure to place thumbs in front.

5. Matching edges, Whipstitch wrong sides of corresponding feet and tail pieces together, stuffing father's tail with fiberfill before closing. Hot glue feet to bottom of corresponding bodies. Center and glue tops of tails to lower body backs.

6. Using tacky glue and matching edges, glue corresponding beak top pieces together, then glue top and bottom pieces to faces.

7. Whipstitch wrong sides of upright iceberg pieces together around sides and top, then Whipstitch sides to bottom, stuffing with fiberfill before closing.

8. Whipstitch wrong sides of fish pieces together, adding a ⅛-inch loop of black yarn to top edge at arrow and a ½-inch loop of black yarn to bottom edge at arrow. Clip bottom loop; trim ends as needed.

Finishing

1. For water, paint top and sides of oval plaque with medium blue acrylic craft paint. While still wet, paint top with light blue, giving it a streaked look. Allow to dry thoroughly. Spray with high-gloss finish. Allow to dry.

2. Using tacky glue, glue blue felt to bottom of plaque and white felt to bottom of floating iceberg.

3. Using photo as a guide through step 8, glue floating iceberg to top of plaque with tacky glue; allow to dry. Hot glue feet and tails of penguins to iceberg.

4. Using tacky glue, attach buttons to father's body front. Glue bow tie button to neck of father or tie ribbon in a bow, trimming ends as desired, then glue in place. Allow to dry.

5. For hats, cut off about a 3-inch cuff from each sock. For each hat, tie cut end closed with yellow sewing thread to make pompom, then roll up other end and glue with fabric glue to secure. Glue hats to heads with tacky glue. Allow to dry.

6. For snowballs, cut seven ½-inch circles from plastic foam. Using fingers, form circles into balls. Using tacky glue through step 9, attach one snowball to bottom of hand on outside arm of each penguin. Glue remaining snowballs in a pile to floating iceberg.

7. Glue upright iceberg to plaque behind floating iceberg and penguins.

8. Glue black cabochons to fish where indicated on graph. Allow to dry.

9. Drill hole in base top for wire. Glue one end of wire into fish bottom and one end into base. Allow to dry thoroughly. Bend wire so fish looks like it is jumping out of water. ❈

COLOR KEY	
Worsted Weight Yarn	**Yards**
☐ White #311	32
▨ Gold #321	11
▨ Light gray #341	17
■ Raspberry #375	2
Uncoded areas are black #312 Continental Stitches	40
╱ Black #312 Overcasting and Whipstitching	
● Attach 4mm black bead	
○ Attach black seed bead	
○ Attach black cabochon	

Color numbers given are for Coats & Clark Red Heart Super Saver worsted weight yarn Art. E300.

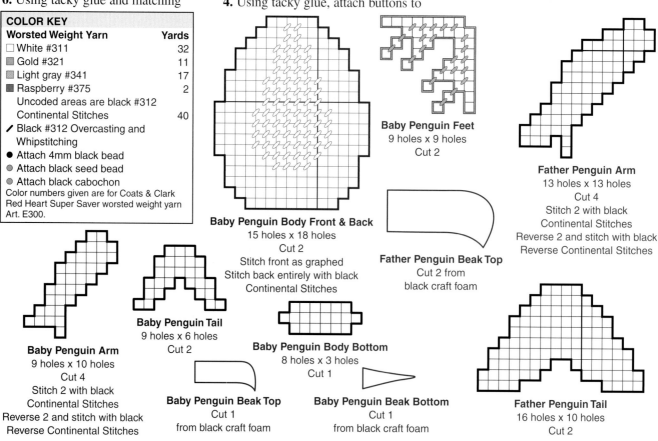

Baby Penguin Feet
9 holes x 9 holes
Cut 2

Father Penguin Arm
13 holes x 13 holes
Cut 4
Stitch 2 with black
Continental Stitches
Reverse 2 and stitch with black
Reverse Continental Stitches

Baby Penguin Body Front & Back
15 holes x 18 holes
Cut 2
Stitch front as graphed
Stitch back entirely with black
Continental Stitches

Father Penguin Beak Top
Cut 2 from
black craft foam

Baby Penguin Tail
9 holes x 6 holes
Cut 2

Baby Penguin Body Bottom
8 holes x 3 holes
Cut 1

Baby Penguin Arm
9 holes x 10 holes
Cut 4
Stitch 2 with black
Continental Stitches
Reverse 2 and stitch with black
Reverse Continental Stitches

Baby Penguin Beak Top
Cut 1
from black craft foam

Baby Penguin Beak Bottom
Cut 1
from black craft foam

Father Penguin Tail
16 holes x 10 holes
Cut 2

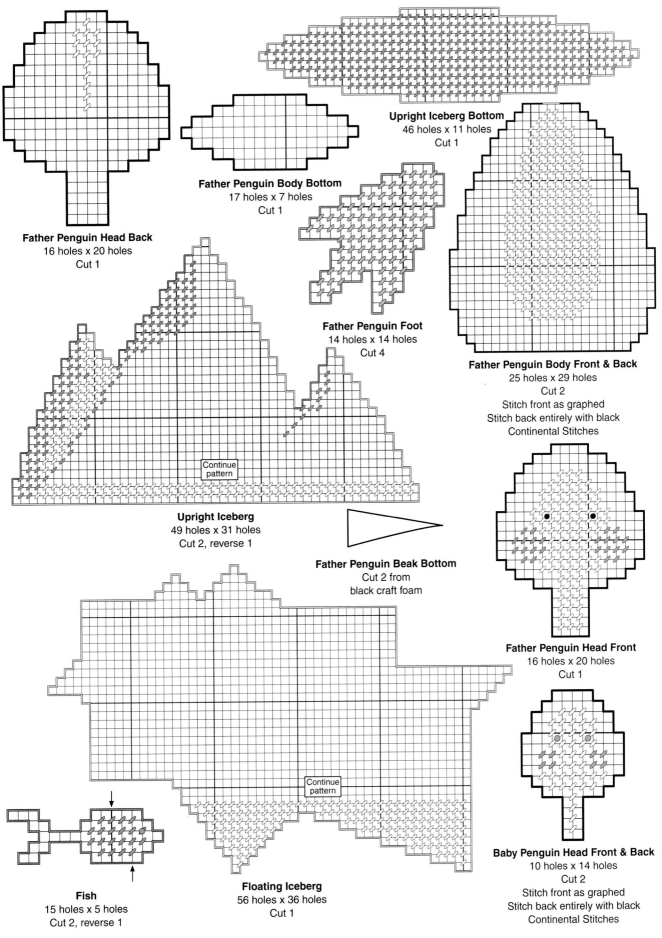

Father Penguin Head Back
16 holes x 20 holes
Cut 1

Father Penguin Body Bottom
17 holes x 7 holes
Cut 1

Upright Iceberg Bottom
46 holes x 11 holes
Cut 1

Father Penguin Foot
14 holes x 14 holes
Cut 4

Father Penguin Body Front & Back
25 holes x 29 holes
Cut 2
Stitch front as graphed
Stitch back entirely with black
Continental Stitches

Continue pattern

Upright Iceberg
49 holes x 31 holes
Cut 2, reverse 1

Father Penguin Beak Bottom
Cut 2 from
black craft foam

Father Penguin Head Front
16 holes x 20 holes
Cut 1

Continue pattern

Fish
15 holes x 5 holes
Cut 2, reverse 1

Floating Iceberg
56 holes x 36 holes
Cut 1

Baby Penguin Head Front & Back
10 holes x 14 holes
Cut 2
Stitch front as graphed
Stitch back entirely with black
Continental Stitches

Sledding Snowman Doorstop

Design by Michele Wilcox

Keep a door open by tucking a brick inside this fun-loving, sled-riding snowman doorstop!

COLOR KEY

Plastic Canvas Yarn	Yards
■ Maple #13	3
■ Dark royal #48	75
■ Mermaid #53	3
☐ Yellow #57	3
Uncoded areas are white #41 Continental Stitches	25
✎ Red #01 Overcasting	5
✎ White #41 Overcasting	

#3 Pearl Cotton

✎ Black #310 Backstitch and Straight Stitch	2
✎ Tangerine #740 Straight Stitch	1
● Black #310 French Knot	

Color numbers given are for Uniek Needloft plastic canvas yarn and DMC #3 pearl cotton.

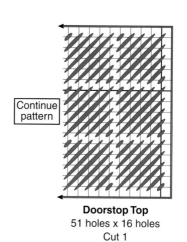

Doorstop Top
51 holes x 16 holes
Cut 1

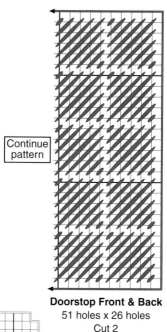

Doorstop Front & Back
51 holes x 26 holes
Cut 2

Doorstop Side
16 holes x 26 holes
Cut 2

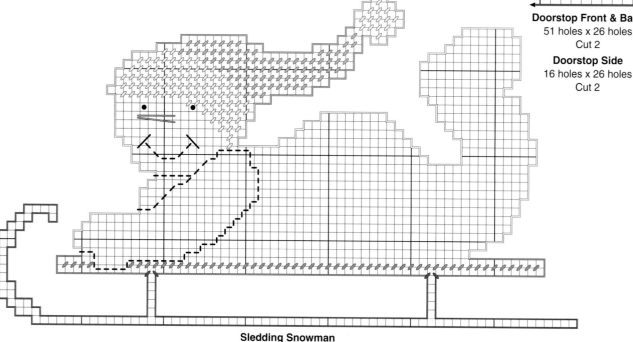

Sledding Snowman
70 holes x 39 holes
Cut 1

Skill Level
Beginner

Materials
- 1½ sheets 7-count plastic canvas
- Uniek Needloft plastic canvas yarn as listed in color key
- #16 tapestry needle
- DMC #3 pearl cotton as listed in color key
- Hot-glue gun

Finished Size
10⅝ inches W x 6⅛ inches H x 2¾ inches D

Instructions
1. Cut plastic canvas according to graphs.

2. Stitch and Overcast sledding snowman following graph, working uncoded area with white Continental Stitches.

3. When background stitching and Overcasting are completed, work pearl cotton embroidery on snowman, filling in nose area between two Straight Stitches shown with tangerine stitches.

4. Stitch doorstop pieces following graphs. Using dark royal throughout, Overcast bottom edges of sides. Whipstitch front and back to sides, then Whipstitch front, back and sides to top.

5. Center and glue snowman to front, making sure bottom edges are even. ❋

Snowman Wind Chime

Design by Kathy Wirth

Hung from your front door or in your kitchen window, this brightly clad little snowman will add tinkling charm to your winter home!

COLOR KEY	
Plastic Canvas Yarn	**Yards**
☐ Pink #07	1
☐ White # 41	11
☐ Bright orange #58	1
■ Bright pink #62	5
■ Bright purple #64	5
Uncoded area on snowman head is white #41 Continental Stitches	
╱ Black #00 Backstitch	1
● Black #00 French Knot	
Metallic Craft Cord	
☐ White/silver #55008	3
◉ Attach wind chime	
Color numbers given are for Uniek Needloft plastic canvas yarn and metallic craft cord.	

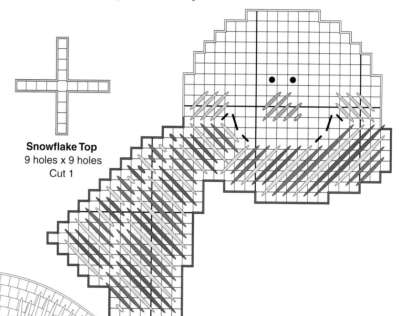

Snowflake Top
9 holes x 9 holes
Cut 1

Snowman Wind Chime Head
33 holes x 29 holes
Cut 1

Snowflake Bottom
7 holes x 7 holes
Cut 1

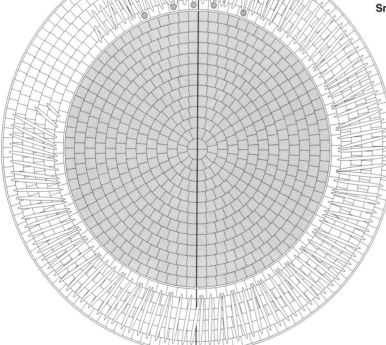

Snowman Wind Chime Body Front & Back
Cut 2,
cutting away gray area
Stitch 1

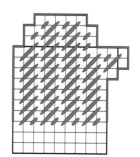

Snowman Wind Chime Mitten
11 holes x 13 holes
Cut 2, reverse 1

Skill Level
Beginner

Finished Size
7⅜ inches W x 8⅜ inches H

Materials
- ½ sheet Uniek QuickCount 7-count plastic canvas
- 2 (6-inch) Uniek QuickShape plastic canvas radial circles
- Uniek Needloft plastic canvas yarn as listed in color key
- Uniek Needloft metallic craft cord as listed in color key
- #16 tapestry needle
- 2 (½-inch) iridescent white pompoms
- 18 inches 19-gauge craft wire
- 10 inches 24-gauge silver craft wire
- Pencil
- 5-piece aluminum wind chimes set
- Wire cutter
- Needle-nose pliers
- Nylon monofilament
- Hot-glue gun

Cutting & Stitching
1. Cut plastic canvas according to graphs, cutting out gray areas of circles.

2. Overcast snowflake pieces with silver metallic craft cord. Stitch remaining pieces following graphs, reversing one mitten before stitching. Work uncoded area on head with white Continental Stitches. Stitch body front only, leaving body back unstitched. *Note: Bottom portion of each mitten is not stitched.*

3. When background stitching is completed, work black yarn Backstitches and French Knots on head with 1 ply yarn.

4. Whipstitch body front and back together with white around both inside and outside edges. Overcast head and mittens following graphs.

Assembly
1. Use photo as a guide throughout assembly. Cut 24-gauge silver wire into five 2-inch lengths. Fold lengths in a "U" shape and insert through holes in chimes.

2. If chimes are different lengths, place longest chime in center and shorter chimes on the outside. Insert wires from front to back through holes indicated on body; twist ends together on back. Apply glue over wire ends on back of body.

3. Glue head to body front over unstitched areas. Glue mittens to body back with thumbs toward the head.

4. With right sides facing up, glue snowflake top to snowflake bottom, placing points of snowflake top between points of snowflake bottom, then glue to lower right side of body.

5. Cut an 18-inch length of white/silver metallic craft cord. Carefully insert 19-gauge wire into cord. To curl, wrap wire around pencil. Bend ends back for safety. Glue ends to head sides, adjusting as needed to fit; glue pompoms over ends.

6. Attach a small hanging loop of nylon filament to center top of head. ✳

Tabletop Decor

Decorate your winter tables with festive snowy decor! End tables, coffee tables and dining tables are perfect for displaying a cheerful centerpiece to lift your winter spirits!

Birdseed Snowman

Design by Nancy Dorman

Don't let the birdseed fool you—this snowman hides a stash of delicious peppermint candy canes behind his back!

Skill Level

Beginner

Finished Size

6¾ inches W x 12 inches H x 3 inches D

Materials

- 1½ sheets Darice Ultra Stiff 7-count plastic canvas
- ½ sheet regular 7-count plastic canvas
- Worsted weight yarn as listed in color key
- ¹⁄₁₆-inch-wide Plastic Canvas 10 Metallic Needlepoint Yarn by Rainbow Gallery as listed in color key
- 6-strand embroidery floss as listed in color key
- #16 tapestry needle
- ¼ yard ⅛-inch-wide green satin ribbon
- ¼ yard ⅛-inch-wide red satin ribbon
- 12 inches ⅛-inch dowel
- Green acrylic craft paint
- Paintbrush
- 6 inches black cloth-covered wire
- Needle-nose pliers (optional)
- Hot-glue gun

Cutting & Stitching

1. Cut snowman and candy cane box pieces from stiff plastic canvas; cut red bird, birdseed bag and birdhouse from regular plastic canvas according to graphs (this page and page 84).

2. Stitch and Overcast snowman, red bird, birdseed bag and birdhouse following graphs, working uncoded areas on snowman with white Continental Stitches and uncoded background on birdseed bag with medium brown Continental Stitches.

3. Work embroidery on snowman with worsted weight yarn and metallic needlepoint yarn, wrapping yarn around needle two times for French Knot eyes and mouth; wrap yarn around needle one time for French Knot buttons, nose and gold berries on hat.

4. Using black embroidery floss throughout, Backstitch letters and lines on birdseed bag. Work French Knot eye on red bird, wrapping floss around needle one time.

5. Stitch candy cane box pieces following graphs. Whipstitch front and back to sides, then Whipstitch front, back and sides to bottom; Overcast top edges.

Finishing

1. Use photo as a guide throughout assembly. Center and glue snowman to candy cane box front, making sure bottom edges are even.

2. For perch, cut toothpick to approximately ¾ inch. Insert ¾-inch length through hole indicated with lavender dot on birdhouse; glue to secure. Tie red ribbon in a bow and glue under perch.

3. For birdhouse post, paint dowel with green acrylic paint. Allow to dry. Glue one end of post to back of birdhouse. Glue bird to roof edge. Glue birdhouse and post to snowman.

4. For handle, thread ends of black cloth-covered wire through holes indicated with red dots on birdseed bag. To secure, wrap ends around wire just above top edge of bag, using needle-nose pliers if desired.

5. Glue bag to snowman. Tie green satin ribbon in a bow; glue to snowman just above center of vest. ❋

COLOR KEY	
Worsted Weight Yarn	**Yards**
■ Green	60
■ Red	10
■ Black	6
▨ Tan	3
■ Dark brown	2
▨ Light gray	1
Uncoded areas on snowman are white Continental Stitches	25
Uncoded background on birdseed bag is medium brown Continental Stitches	6
⁄ Yellow Overcasting	1
⁄ White Overcasting	
⁄ Medium brown Overcasting	
⁄ Green Backstitch and Straight Stitch	
● Orange French Knot	1
● Black French Knot	
¹⁄₁₆-Inch Metallic Needlepoint Yarn	
⁄ Gold #PM51 Straight Stitch	1
○ Gold #PM51 French Knot	
6-Strand Embroidery Floss	
⁄ Black Backstitch and Straight Stitch	2
● Black French Knot	
Color numbers given are for Rainbow Gallery Plastic Canvas 10 Metallic Needlepoint Yarn.	

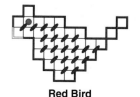

Red Bird
11 holes x 7 holes
Cut 1 from regular

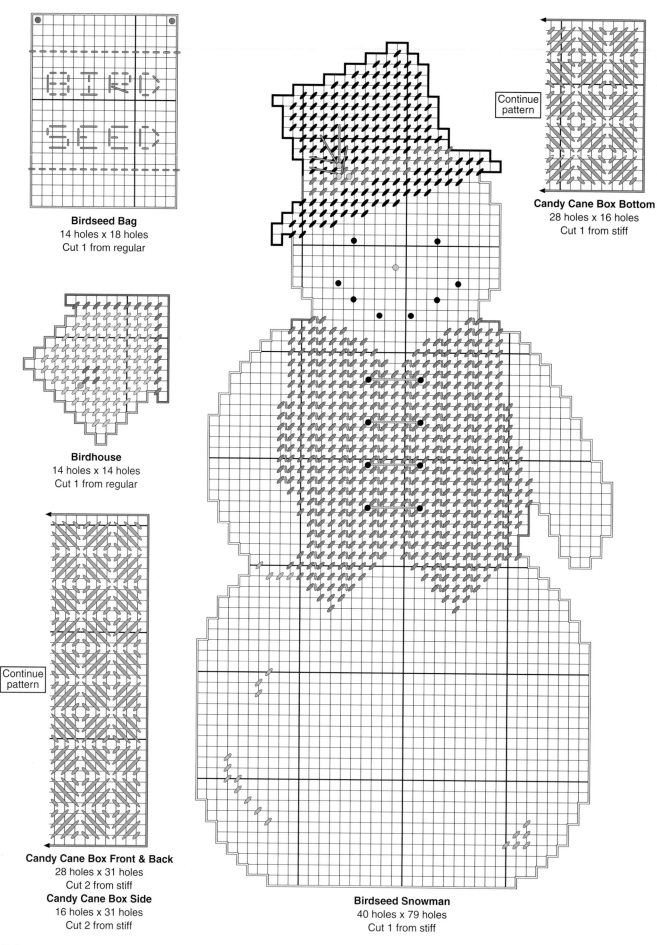

Birdseed Bag
14 holes x 18 holes
Cut 1 from regular

Birdhouse
14 holes x 14 holes
Cut 1 from regular

Continue
pattern

Candy Cane Box Front & Back
28 holes x 31 holes
Cut 2 from stiff

Candy Cane Box Side
16 holes x 31 holes
Cut 2 from stiff

Continue
pattern

Candy Cane Box Bottom
28 holes x 16 holes
Cut 1 from stiff

Birdseed Snowman
40 holes x 79 holes
Cut 1 from stiff

84 *Let It Snow! in Plastic Canvas*

Cozy Coaster-Chair Set

Designs by Ronda Bryce

Stitch this soft and cozy armchair to house six unique "afghan" coasters to protect your coffee table.

Skill Level

Advanced

Finished Size

Armchair: 7⅝ inches W x 9 inches H x 5¼ inches D

Afghan coasters: 4½ inches W x 5 inches L

Pillow: 2½ inches square

Crocheted rug: 3¾ inches W x 5⅝ inches L

Materials

- 4 sheets 7-count plastic canvas
- 2 (3-inch) Uniek QuickShape plastic canvas radial circles
- Uniek Needloft plastic canvas yarn: 20 yards beige #40 (for crocheted afghan) and as listed in color key
- Lion Chenille Sensations acrylic yarn from Lion Brand Yarn Co. as listed in color key
- #16 tapestry needle
- 2-inch white fabric and Battenburg square doily #016-2SQ from Wimpole Street Creations
- 2 (3-inch) white fabric and Battenburg square doilies #016-3SQ from Wimpole Street Creations
- Sewing needle and white sewing thread
- Size H/8 crochet hook
- 2¼-inch gold wire-frame doll eyeglasses #7644 from Fibre-Craft Materials Corp. (optional)
- Polyester fiberfill

Cutting & Stitching

1. Cut plastic canvas according to graphs. Cut two 37-hole x 33-hole pieces for base top and bottom. Base top and bottom will remain unstitched.

2. For arm front, cut and discard five outer rows of holes from both 3-inch plastic canvas radial circles. Continental Stitch each round with russet, working a Cross Stitch in center.

3. Stitch remaining pieces following graphs. Using Blanket Stitch (see diagram on page 87), Overcast afghans A and B with gold, afghans C and D with beige and afghans E and F with black.

4. Using beige, Whipstitch wrong sides of pillow pieces together with Blanket Stitch, stuffing with a small amount of fiberfill before closing.

Chair Assembly

1. *Base:* Using russet throughout assembly, Whipstitch base back to base sides, then Whipstitch unstitched base top and bottom to back and sides. Overcast around sides and bottom of base front, then Whipstitch top edge of front to remaining unworked edge of base top. Set aside.

2. *Chair back:* Whipstitch chair top and bottom to chair sides along short edges, forming a square. Whipstitch the two chair back pieces to remaining edges of square.

3. *Seat cushion:* Repeat step for chair back using cushion pieces.

4. *Chair arms:* Whipstitch side edges on one arm piece together, forming a circle. Whipstitch one chair front to one end of chair arm. Repeat with remaining arm and arm front.

5. Using photo as a guide through step 8, place chair back on seat cushion, so that back part of cushion and chair back are aligned. Whipstitch together at bottom corners of chair back.

6. To complete chair top, place chair arms on top sides of seat cushion; tack to cushion in about every fourth hole.

7. Place chair top on chair base, making sure to place flap on base in front; tack in place all around in about every fourth hole.

8. Using sewing needle and white sewing thread, tack 2-inch doily to center top of seat back; tack one 3-inch doily to each arm.

9. Store afghan coasters inside base.

Crocheted Rug

Row 1: With beige, ch 20, sc in 2nd ch from hook and in each rem ch across, ch 1, turn. (19 sc)

Rows 2–13: Sc in each sc across, ch 1, turn.

Row 14: Sc in each sc across, fasten off.

Arrange pillow, crocheted rug and eyeglasses as desired. ✻

COLOR KEY	
Chenille Acrylic Yarn	**Yards**
■ Russet	163
Plastic Canvas Yarn	
■ Black #00	26
■ Red #01	7
▨ Burgundy #03	7
▨ Rust #09	11
☐ Gold #17	18
■ Forest #29	8
☐ Beige #40	11
■ Purple #46	7
▨ Dark royal #48	8
Color numbers given are for Lion Brand Lion Chenille Sensations acrylic yarn and Uniek Needloft plastic canvas yarn.	

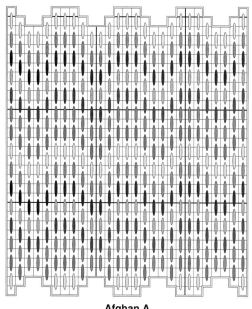

Afghan A
27 holes x 31 holes
Cut 1

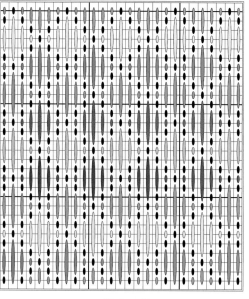

Afghan B
27 holes x 31 holes
Cut 1

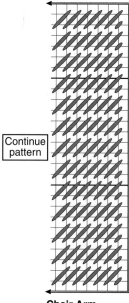

Continue pattern

Chair Arm
29 holes x 27 holes
Cut 2

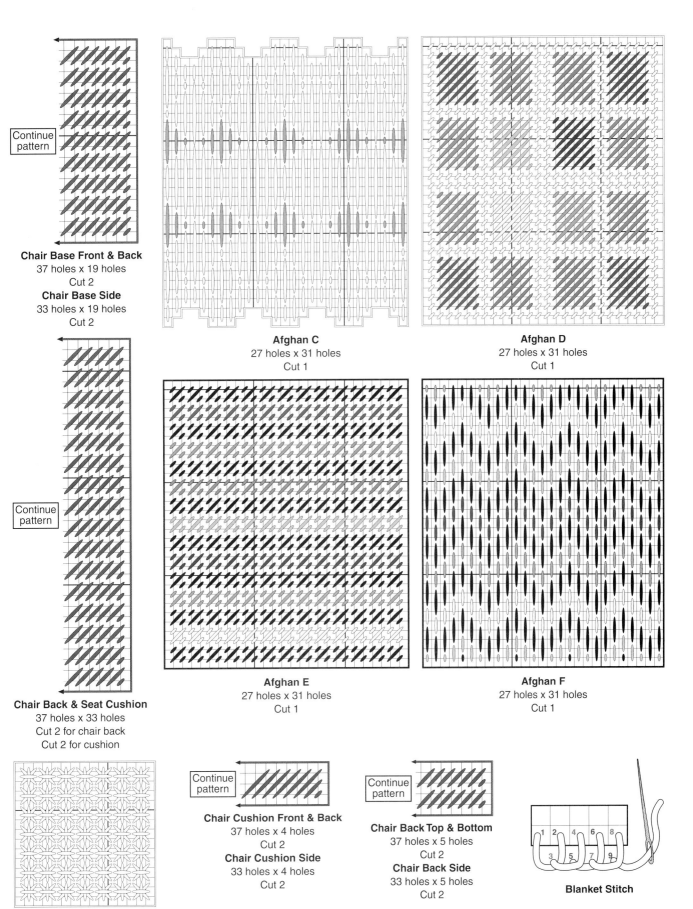

Chair Base Front & Back
37 holes x 19 holes
Cut 2

Chair Base Side
33 holes x 19 holes
Cut 2

Continue pattern

Afghan C
27 holes x 31 holes
Cut 1

Afghan D
27 holes x 31 holes
Cut 1

Continue pattern

Chair Back & Seat Cushion
37 holes x 33 holes
Cut 2 for chair back
Cut 2 for cushion

Afghan E
27 holes x 31 holes
Cut 1

Afghan F
27 holes x 31 holes
Cut 1

Pillow
15 holes x 15 holes
Cut 2

Continue pattern

Chair Cushion Front & Back
37 holes x 4 holes
Cut 2

Chair Cushion Side
33 holes x 4 holes
Cut 2

Continue pattern

Chair Back Top & Bottom
37 holes x 5 holes
Cut 2

Chair Back Side
33 holes x 5 holes
Cut 2

Blanket Stitch

Snow Chef

Design by Joan Green

Stand this snowman in your kitchen or stitch him without the back piece and glue to a large bottle or bag to dress up a special gift!

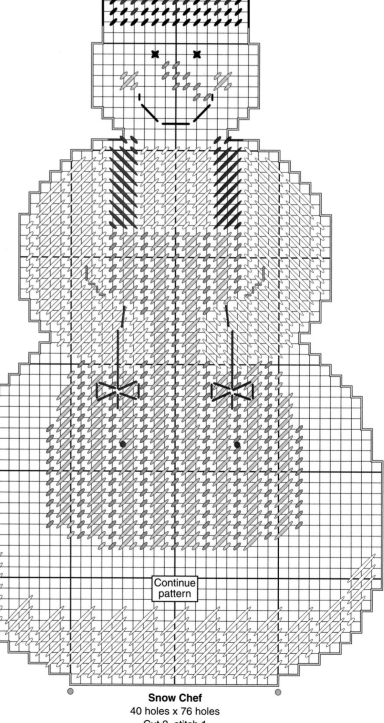

Snow Chef
40 holes x 76 holes
Cut 2, stitch 1

Skill Level

Beginner

Finished Size

6 inches W x 11⅜ inches H without the stand

Materials

- 1 sheet 7-count plastic canvas
- Coats & Clark Red Heart Classic worsted weight yarn Art. E267 as listed in color key
- Coats & Clark Red Heart Kids worsted weight yarn Art. E711 as listed in color key
- #16 tapestry needle
- 8 inches ⅛-inch-wide red satin ribbon
- 2 Mill Hill Products ceramic Debbie Mumm Gingerbread Man with Bow Tie buttons #43019 from Gay Bowles Sales Inc.
- 7½-inch-tall white doll stand #7381 from Fibre-Craft Materials Corp.
- Sheet white felt
- Sewing needle and red sewing thread
- Fabric glue

Instructions

1. Cut front and back from plastic canvas according to graphs. Back will remain unstitched. Using snow chef as a template, cut felt slightly smaller all around.

2. Stitch front following graph, working uncoded areas with white Continental Stitches. Backstitch mouth with black, hangers for gingerbread man buttons with cherry red and lines on chef's hat and arms with nickel.

3. Using sewing needle and red sewing thread, attach buttons where indicated on graph; knot thread ends and weave in to secure.

4. Overcast bottom edge of front from dot to dot with silver. Following graph, Whipstitch back to front along remaining edges.

5. Tie red ribbon in a bow trimming ends as desired. Glue to neck area. Glue felt to back.

6. Discard ring portion of doll stand, then slip snow chef over stand for display, placing base of stand behind snow chef. ❊

Hot Chocolate Set

Design by Kathy Wirth

There's nothing like hot chocolate on a cold, snowy day. Leave this welcoming tote, mug and coaster set on the table for your family members to help themselves to a warm treat!

Skill Level
Beginner

Finished Size
Tote: 3¾ inches W x 5⅞ inches H x 1⅛ inches D

Mug insert: 3½ inches H x 3⅓ inches in diameter

Coaster: 4 inches x 4 inches

Materials
- 2 sheets Uniek QuickCount 7-count plastic canvas
- 2 (6-inch) Uniek QuickShape plastic canvas hearts
- Uniek Needloft plastic canvas yarn as listed in color key
- Uniek Needloft metallic craft cord as listed in color key
- #16 tapestry needle
- Sheet white adhesive-backed Presto felt by Kunin Felt
- 18 inches ⅝-inch-wide sheer white ribbon
- White-rimmed Mugs Your Way acrylic mug with insert by Crafter's Pride from Daniel Enterprises

Instructions
1. Cut plastic canvas according to graphs, cutting away gray areas on plastic canvas hearts for tote front and back. Also cut one 24-hole x 11-hole piece for tote bottom. Tote bottom will remain unstitched.

2. Cut four 3½-inch circles from felt. Set aside.

3. Stitch pieces following graphs,

working uncoded areas with royal Continental Stitches and leaving four coaster pieces unstitched.

4. Using solid silver, Overcast inside edges and handle edges on tote front and back; Overcast top edges on sides. Using royal, Whipstitch front and back to sides, then Whipstitch front, back and sides to unstitched bottom.

5. Tie sheer ribbon in a small bow around handle as in photo.

6. Using royal, Whipstitch one unstitched coaster each to one stitched coaster. Remove backing from felt circles and apply to unstitched backs of coasters.

7. Using royal, Whipstitch side edges of mug insert together, forming a cylinder; Overcast top and bottom edges.

8. Following manufacturer's instructions, place stitched insert in mug, aligning seam with handle. ✳

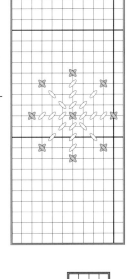

Hot Chocolate Tote Side
11 holes x 24 holes
Cut 2

COLOR KEY

Plastic Canvas Yarn	Yards
▨ Royal #32	90
☐ White #41	32

Uncoded areas are royal #32 Continental Stitches

Metallic Craft Cord

	Yards
▨ Solid silver #55021	17

Color numbers given are for Uniek Needloft plastic canvas yarn and metallic craft cord.

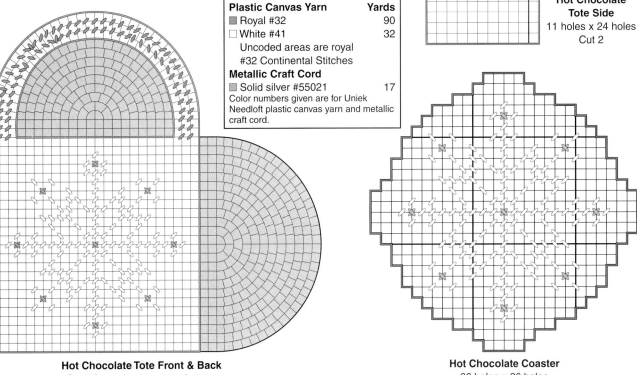

Hot Chocolate Tote Front & Back
Cut 2 from plastic canvas hearts,
cutting away gray areas

Hot Chocolate Coaster
26 holes x 26 holes
Cut 8, stitch 4

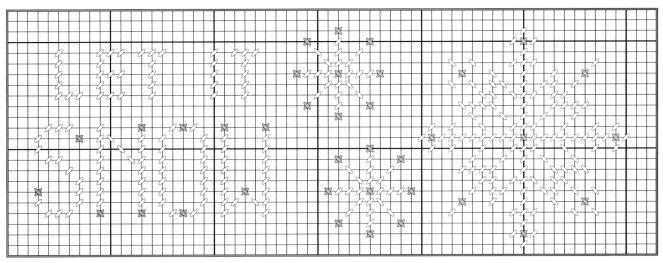

Hot Chocolate Mug Insert
63 holes x 23 holes
Cut 1

It's Snow Time!

Design by Judy Collishaw

A miniature clock transforms this snowy stitched scene into a wintry timepiece!

COLOR KEY

Worsted Weight Yarn	Yards
■ Denim blue	13
□ White	9
○ White French Knot	
Sport Weight Yarn	
▨ Kelly green	4
■ Red	1
□ Yellow	1
■ Black	1
▨ Forest green	1
Uncoded areas on snowman are white Continental Stitches	3
⁄ White Overcasting	
⁄ Gray Backstitch and Overcasting	2
⁄ Orange Straight Stitch	1
#5 Pearl Cotton	
⁄ Black #310 Backstitch	1
⁄ Light steel gray #318 Backstitch and Straight Stitch	1
● Attach 3mm black bead	

Color numbers given are for DMC #5 pearl cotton.

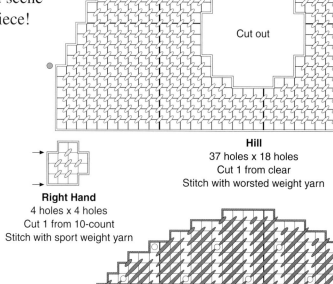

Hill
37 holes x 18 holes
Cut 1 from clear
Stitch with worsted weight yarn

Right Hand
4 holes x 4 holes
Cut 1 from 10-count
Stitch with sport weight yarn

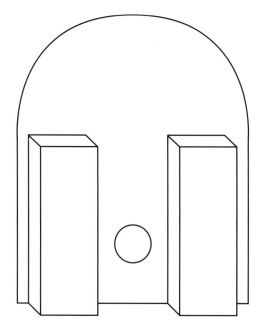

Fig. 1

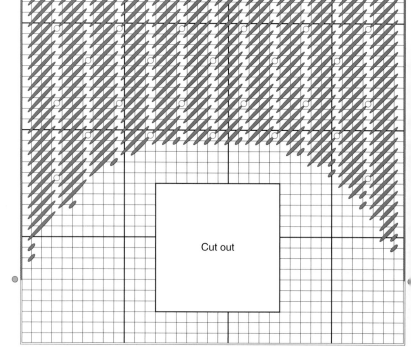

Backdrop
37 holes x 47 holes
Cut 1 from 7-count
Stitch with worsted weight yarn

Beginner

Finished Size

5⅝ inches W x 7⅛ inches H x 1¼ inches D

Materials

- 1½ sheets 7-count plastic canvas
- ½ sheet 10-count plastic canvas
- Worsted weight yarn as listed in color key
- Sport weight yarn as listed in color key
- DMC #5 pearl cotton as listed in color key
- #16 tapestry needle
- #18 tapestry needle
- 1⁷⁄₁₆ in diameter x ¼ inch deep clock insert movement
- 2 (3mm) round black beads
- Sewing needle and black sewing thread
- 2 round toothpicks
- 2 (⅜-inch) silver snap fasteners
- ¼-inch yellow pompom
- ½ cup rice or aquarium gravel
- 2 small zip-top plastic bags
- Low-temperature glue gun

Cutting & Stitching

1. Cut backdrop and hill from 7-count plastic canvas according to graphs. Cut eight 9-hole x 24-hole pieces for weight box sides and four 9-hole x 9-hole pieces for weight box ends from 7-count plastic canvas. Weight box pieces will remain unstitched.

2. Cut skiing snowman, right hand, left arm and skis from 10-count plastic canvas according to graphs (pages 92 and 95).

3. Following graphs through step 8 and using #16 tapestry needle and worsted weight yarn through step 5, stitch top part of backdrop with denim blue, then Overcast around sides and top from dot to dot. Using 2 plies white worsted weight yarn, work French Knots for falling snow.

4. For hill, Overcast inside edges, then

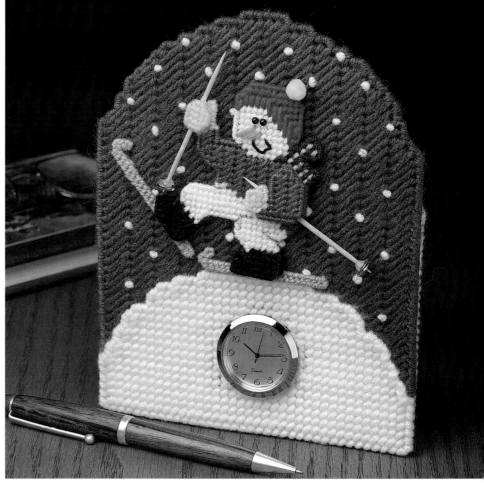

top edges from dot to dot. Place hill on backdrop, aligning bottom and side edges, then Continental Stitch with white through both thicknesses.

5. With white, Whipstitch hill and backdrop together around side and bottom edges from dot to dot.

6. Using #18 tapestry needle and sport weight yarn through step 7, stitch and Overcast 10-count pieces, leaving edges between arrows on snowman and right hand unstitched.

7. With right sides facing up, place right hand over hand on snowman, then Whipstitch together along unstitched edges.

8. Straight Stitch nose with orange yarn and Backstitch mouth with black pearl cotton. For eyes, using sewing needle and black sewing thread, attach 3mm black beads to head where indicated on graph.

Assembly

1. Use photo as a guide throughout assembly. Glue skis to bottom backside of feet. Glue snowman to backdrop, with bottom ski resting on top edge of hill. Glue pompom to tip of hat.

2. For ski poles, insert tip of a toothpick through hole on bottom half of each snap; glue to secure. With snaps at bottom, glue one toothpick between layers of right hand; glue remaining toothpick under left arm, then glue arm to body under scarf, aligning outside edges.

3. For each weight box, using white worsted weight yarn, Whipstitch long edges of four box sides together, then Whipstitch bottom end to box sides. Fill a zip-top plastic bag with half of rice or aquarium gravel; close bag. Stuff bag into weight box; Whipstitch top end to box.

4. Stand boxes on end against wrong side of backdrop on each side of clock opening. Making sure bottom edges are even, center and glue boxes between opening and side edges of backdrop (Fig. 1).

5. Place clock in hole. ✻

Graphs continued on page 95

Snowflake Basket

Design by Marianne Telesca

Filled with your favorite candies or an arrangement of frosted pinecones and pine boughs, this easy-to-stitch basket makes a lovely winter decoration.

Materials

- 1 artist-size sheet of 7-count plastic canvas
- 2 (6-inch) Uniek QuickShape plastic canvas hearts
- 4 (5-inch) Uniek QuickShape plastic canvas hexagons
- Uniek Needloft plastic canvas yarn as listed in color key
- Plastic Canvas 7 Metallic Needlepoint Yarn by Rainbow Gallery as listed in color key
- #16 tapestry needle
- 17-inch piece craft wire
- Hot-glue gun

Skill Level

Beginner

Finished Size

9 inches W x 8½ inches H x 4 inches D

Instructions

1. Cut plastic canvas according to graphs, cutting away gray areas on plastic canvas hearts and hexagons.

2. Stitch and Overcast handle and snowflakes following graphs.

3. Stitch basket side, overlapping three holes on short ends as indicated on graph and stitching through both layers of plastic canvas.

4. Holding craft wire along one long edge of side, Overcast this edge with sail blue, covering both edge and wire. The wire-reinforced edge becomes top of basket.

5. Overlap 18 holes of two unstitched bottom pieces where indicated on graph. Centering basket seam along this overlap, Whipstitch basket bottom to bottom edge of basket with sail blue, easing around curves as necessary.

6. Using photo as a guide, glue ends of handle inside basket. Glue one snowflake to each side and each end of basket. ✻

Basket Bottom
Cut 2 from plastic canvas hearts,
cutting away gray area
Do not stitch

COLOR KEY

Plastic Canvas Yarn	Yards
■ Sail blue #35	17
□ White #41	24
Metallic Needlepoint Yarn	
■ Silver #PC2	32
■ White pearl #PC10	12

Color numbers given are for Uniek Needloft plastic canvas yarn and Rainbow Gallery Plastic Canvas 7 Metallic Needlepoint Yarn.

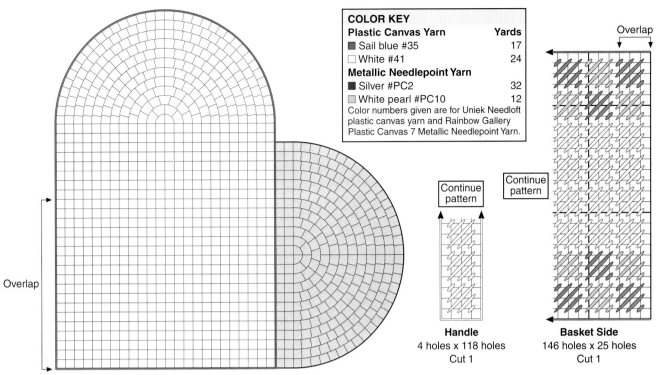

Continue pattern

Continue pattern

Overlap

Handle
4 holes x 118 holes
Cut 1

Basket Side
146 holes x 25 holes
Cut 1

Snowflake
Cut 4 from plastic canvas hexagons,
cutting away gray areas

It's Snow Time!

Continued from page 93

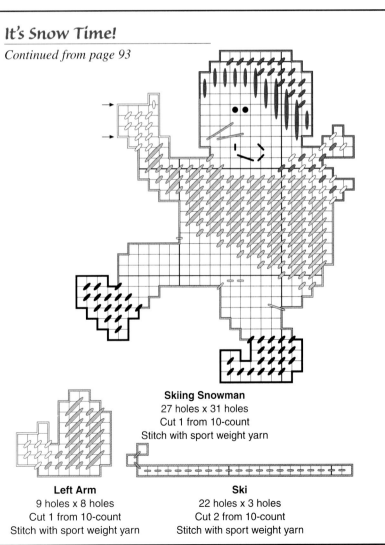

Skiing Snowman
27 holes x 31 holes
Cut 1 from 10-count
Stitch with sport weight yarn

Left Arm
9 holes x 8 holes
Cut 1 from 10-count
Stitch with sport weight yarn

Ski
22 holes x 3 holes
Cut 2 from 10-count
Stitch with sport weight yarn

Quilted Snowman

Design by Janelle Giese

 dding metallic braid stitches to this snowman gives him an eye-catching glittery look perfect for the holidays!

Skill Level

Intermediate

Finished Size

8⅜ inches W x 11½ inches H x 2¼ inches D

Materials

- 2 sheets Uniek QuickCount stiff 7-count plastic canvas
- Uniek Needloft plastic canvas yarn as listed in color key
- Kreinik Heavy (#32) Braid as listed in color key
- DMC #5 pearl cotton as listed in color key
- DMC #8 pearl cotton as listed in color key
- #16 tapestry needle
- ¼-inch white acrylic pompom
- 1¼-inch silver eye pin
- Toothpick or wooden skewer
- Pliers
- Thick white glue

Cutting & Stitching

1. Cut one bunny, two snowmen, two base pieces and two reinforcements from plastic canvas according to graphs (this page and page 98). Reinforcements will remain unstitched.

2. Following graphs through step 7, stitch and Overcast bunny, working uncoded area with white Continental Stitches.

3. Place snowman pieces together and base pieces together; stitch each as one, working uncoded areas with white Continental Stitches and leaving blue, green and red Whipstitch lines

unworked at this time

4. Whipstitch around sides and top of snowman, leaving bottom edges unworked. Whipstitch around base edges.

5. Using pearl heavy (#32) braid throughout, work Straight Stitches and Cross Stitches on snowman. For Pin Stitches on eyes, bring braid up in hole indicated below stitch, go down through black yarn, splitting stitch, then back through same hole in which stitch originated.

6. Using full strands white and lilac yarn, work Straight Stitches on hatband. Using black #5 pearl cotton, work remaining embroidery on snowman.

7. Use 1 ply lavender yarn to work Straight Stitch over bunny's eye. Using black #8 pearl cotton, work remaining embroidery on bunny.

Assembly

1. Use photo as a guide throughout assembly. Using white yarn through step 2, Whipstitch reinforcements to snowman with Continental Stitches along green Whipstitch lines, using colors indicated.

2. Whipstitch bottom edges of snowman to blue Whipstitch line on base; Whipstitch reinforcements to base matching red Whipstitch lines.

3. Glue white pompom to bunny for tail. For needle, using pliers, squeeze round end of eye pin so it resembles the eye of a needle. Insert other end through stitches on backside of bunny's front paws.

4. Tack bunny to base with two small flesh tone stitches, then secure to base

with a thick line of glue along bottom edge behind bunny.

5. For quilting thread, thread remaining length of black #8 pearl cotton through eye of needle. Arrange "thread" as desired, then use toothpick or skewer to dab glue at various points to hold in place. ✳

Quilted Snowman Reinforcement
3 holes x 6 holes
Cut 2
Do not stitch

COLOR KEY	
Plastic Canvas Yarn	**Yards**
■ Black #00	1
■ Lavender #05	2
□ Pink #07	2
□ Tangerine #11	1
■ Pumpkin #12	1
■ Sail blue #35	3
□ Baby blue #36	17
□ Lilac #45	4
■ Purple #46	4
□ Mermaid #53	3
□ Flesh tone #56	2
Uncoded areas are white #41 Continental Stitches	41
⁄ White #41 Straight Stitch and Whipstitching	
⁄ Lavender #05 Straight Stitch	
⁄ Lilac #45 Straight Stitch	
Heavy (#32) Braid	
⁄ Pearl #032 Straight Stitch, Cross Stitch and Pin Stitch	9
#5 Pearl Cotton	
⁄ Black #310 Backstitch, Straight Stitch and Running Stitch	5
#8 Pearl Cotton	
⁄ Black #310 Backstitch and Straight Stitch	1
Color numbers given are for Uniek Needloft plastic canvas yarn, Kreinik Heavy (#32) Braid and DMC #5 and #8 pearl cotton.	

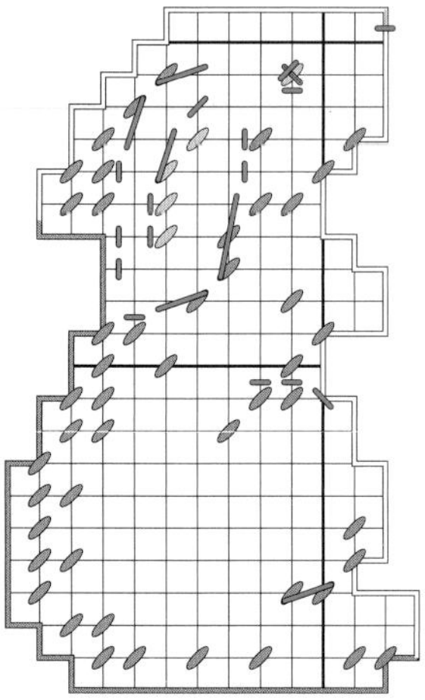

Quilted Snowman Bunny
13 holes x 21 holes
Cut 1

Quilted Snowman
55 holes x 75 holes
Cut 2, stitch as 1

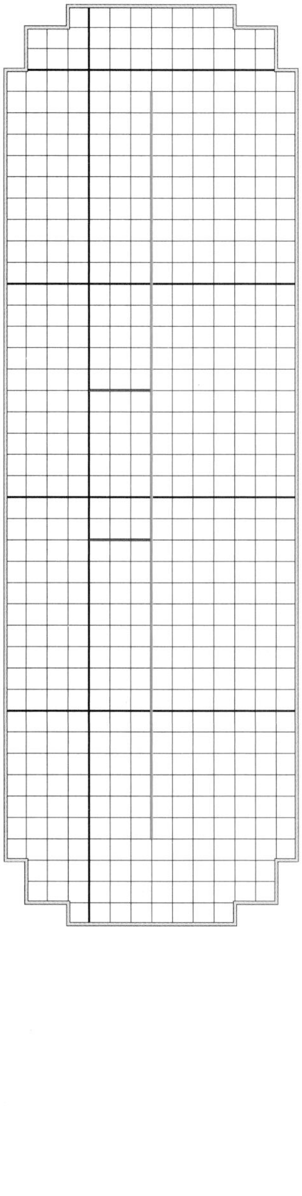

Quilted Snowman Base
43 holes x 14 holes
Cut 2, stitch as 1

Snowy Brick Cottage

Design by Angie Arickx

Transform a plain tissue box into a winter escape with this cozy brick-red cottage!

Skill Level
Beginner

Finished Size
Fits regular-size tissue box

Materials
- 1 artist-size sheet Uniek Quick-Count 7-count plastic canvas
- Uniek Needloft plastic canvas yarn as listed in color key
- #16 tapestry needle
- Hot-glue gun

Instructions
1. Cut plastic canvas according to graphs (pages 100 and 101).

2. Stitch pieces following graphs, working uncoded areas on all roof, chimney and tree pieces with white Continental Stitches and uncoded areas on cottage front, back and sides with burgundy Continental Stitches.

3. Follow graphs through step 7. When background stitching is completed, work burgundy Backstitches on chimney pieces and black French Knots on doors.

4. Overcast trees and bushes. Overcast top edges of chimney pieces, then Whipstitch together along side edges. Whipstitch cottage sides to front and back; Overcast top and bottom edges.

5. Overcast around side and bottom edges of roof trim pieces from dot to dot. Overcast vertical edges only of

chimney openings on roof sides.

6. Use photo as a guide through step 8. Whipstitch top edges of roof sides together, then Whipstitch bottom edges of two opposite sides of chimney to opening on roof sides. Bottom edges of remaining two chimney sides will not be stitched.

7. Whipstitch top edges of trim long sides to bottom edges of roof sides. Whipstitch top edges of trim short sides to roof side edges.

8. Center and glue one tree to each cottage side. Glue bushes to front and back. Place roof on cottage and secure with glue. ❋

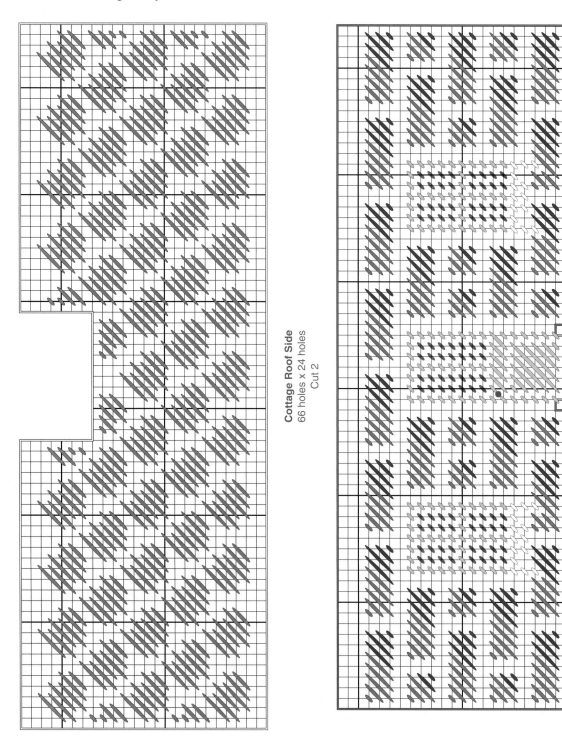

Cottage Roof Side
66 holes x 24 holes
Cut 2

Cottage Front & Back
64 holes x 22 holes
Cut 2

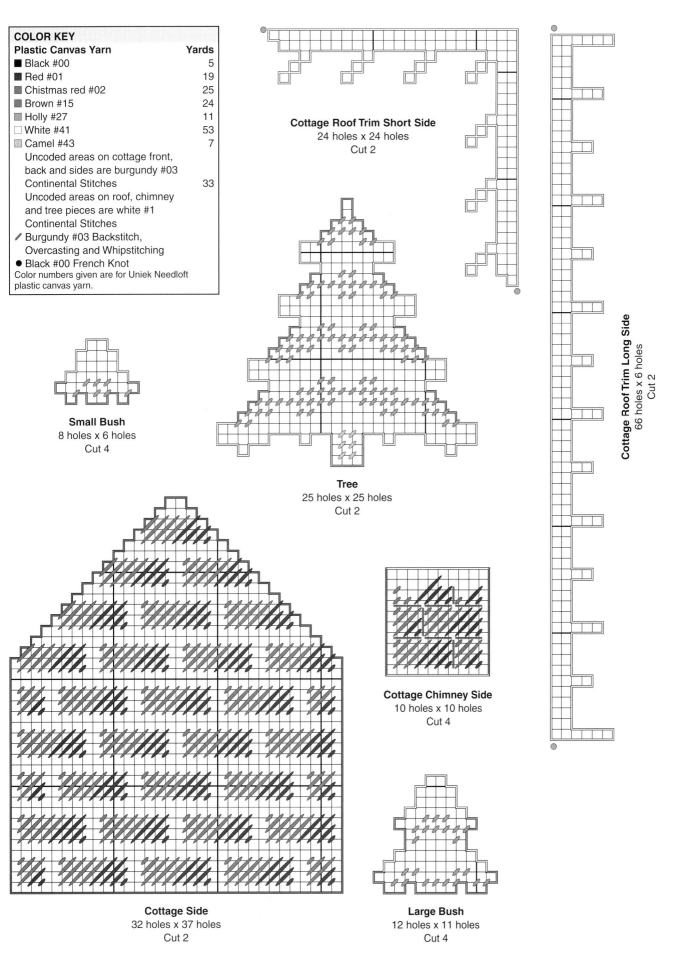

COLOR KEY

Plastic Canvas Yarn	Yards
■ Black #00	5
■ Red #01	19
■ Chistmas red #02	25
■ Brown #15	24
■ Holly #27	11
□ White #41	53
■ Camel #43	7

Uncoded areas on cottage front, back and sides are burgundy #03 Continental Stitches   33

Uncoded areas on roof, chimney and tree pieces are white #1 Continental Stitches

✓ Burgundy #03 Backstitch, Overcasting and Whipstitching

● Black #00 French Knot

Color numbers given are for Uniek Needloft plastic canvas yarn.

Cottage Roof Trim Short Side
24 holes x 24 holes
Cut 2

Cottage Roof Trim Long Side
66 holes x 6 holes
Cut 2

Small Bush
8 holes x 6 holes
Cut 4

Tree
25 holes x 25 holes
Cut 2

Cottage Chimney Side
10 holes x 10 holes
Cut 4

Cottage Side
32 holes x 37 holes
Cut 2

Large Bush
12 holes x 11 holes
Cut 4

Snowman & Snow Lady

Designs by Judy Collishaw

Stitch this adorable snow couple to hold sugary treats or a small gift for a party guest!

Materials

- 1 sheet 7-count plastic canvas
- Worsted weight yarn as listed in color key
- DMC #5 pearl cotton as listed in color key
- #16 tapestry needle
- ½-inch white pompom
- Low-temperature glue gun

Skill Level

Beginner

Finished Size

Snowman: 2⅞ inches W x 6½ inches H x 2⅛ inches D

Snowlady: 2⅞ inches W x 6 inches H x 2⅛ inches D

Cutting & Stitching

1. Cut plastic canvas according to graphs. Base will remain unstitched.

2. Stitch heads, backs and feet following graphs, working uncoded area on each head with white Continental Stitches. When background stitching is completed, work embroidery on heads. Overcast heads and feet.

3. Work snowman front as graphed. Work snowlady front reversing red and kelly green.

4. Stitch and Overcast snowman's

COLOR KEY

Worsted Weight Yarn	Yards
☐ White	14
◼ Red	10
☐ Kelly green	9
◼ Forest green	9
Uncoded areas on heads are white Continental Stitches	
⟋ Orange Straight Stitch	1
● Black French Knot	1
#5 Pearl Cotton	
⟋ Black #310 Backstitch	1
⟋ Red #321 Backstitch	1
Color numbers given are for DMC #5 pearl cotton.	

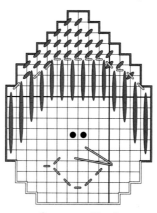

Snowman Head
14 holes x 18 holes
Cut 1

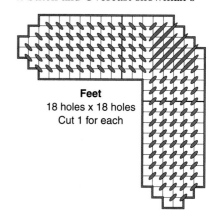

Feet
18 holes x 18 holes
Cut 1 for each

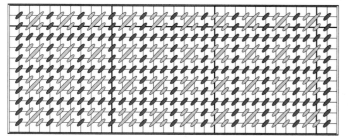

Snowman & Snow Lady Front
32 holes x 12 holes
Cut 1 for each
Stitch snowman front as graphed
Stitch snow lady front,
reversing red and kelly green

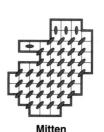

Mitten
8 holes x 9 holes
Cut 2, reverse 1, for each
Stitch snowman's mittens as graphed
Stitch snow lady's mittens,
reversing red and forest green

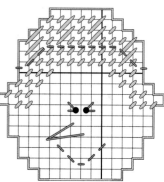

Snow Lady Head
16 holes x 16 holes
Cut 1

mittens following graph, reversing one before stitching. Stitch and Overcast snowlady's mittens, reversing red and forest green yarn and reversing one mitten before stitching.

5. Overcast top edges of front. Overcast back pieces around sides and top from top dot on one side to top dot on other side.

Assembly

1. Use photo as a guide throughout assembly. Whipstitch bottom edge of snowman front to base around curved edge with red. Repeat for snowlady using kelly green.

2. For each snow person, using white throughout, Whipstitch side edges of front to back from dot to dot; Whipstitch back edge of base to bottom edge of back.

3. Working with corresponding pieces and adjacent mitten colors for each, tack mittens with thumbs up to back at arrows. Glue mittens along top edge of front.

4. Glue heads to top front of backs. Glue feet to base, allowing ¾ inches of shoes to protrude from front. *Note: About ¼ inch of feet will be showing in the back.*

5. For snowman, cut two 12-inch lengths each of red and kelly green yarn. Place lengths side by side, twist together slightly and tie in a knot around neck for scarf. Glue pompom to top of hat.

6. For snowlady, tie a 6-inch length of kelly green in a bow; glue under chin, for bonnet tie. ✳

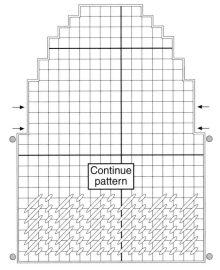

Snowman & Snow Lady Back
18 holes x 24 holes
Cut 1 for each

Continue pattern

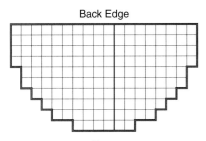

Back Edge

Base
18 holes x 10 holes
Cut 1 for each
Do not stitch
Whipstitch to snowman
following graph
Whipstitch to snow lady,
substituting forest green for red

Snow People

Designs by Angie Arickx

This cuddly snow family set makes it easy to redecorate your home for the cold months!

Skill Level

Beginner

Finished Size

Birdhouse tissue topper: Fits boutique-size tissue box

Napkin holder: 7¼ inches W x 4 inches H x 2½ inches D

Snowman magnet: 2¼ inches W x 3⅛ inches H

Snow woman magnet: 2¼ inches W x 3 inches H

Snow child magnet: 1⅞ inches W x 2½ inches H

Materials

- 1½ artist-size sheets Uniek QuickCount 7-count plastic canvas
- Uniek Needloft plastic canvas yarn as listed in color key
- #16 tapestry needle
- 3 (1-inch) lengths magnetic strip
- Hot-glue gun

Birdhouse Tissue Topper

1. Cut plastic canvas according to graphs (pages 106 and 107), cutting four of each snowman and snow woman.

2. Following graphs through step 8, stitch and Overcast snow people, shutters and perches, working uncoded areas with white Continental Stitches and leaving one short edge of each perch unstitched.

3. When background stitching is completed, work black Backstitches and French Knots on snow people.

4. Stitch remaining pieces following graphs, working uncoded areas on birdhouse front, back and sides with white Continental Stitches.

5. Overcast top edges of chimney pieces, then Whipstitch together along side edges. With camel, Whipstitch unstitched edges of perches to front and back where indicated with red line. Whipstitch birdhouse front and back to sides; Overcast top and bottom edges.

6. Use photo as a guide through step 9. Overcast bottom edges of roof sides. Overcast vertical edges only of chimney openings on roof sides.

7. Whipstitch top edges of roof sides together, then Whipstitch bottom edges of two opposite sides of chimney to opening on roof sides. Bottom edges of remaining two chimney sides will not be stitched.

8. Overcast around side and bottom edges of trim pieces from dot to dot. Whipstitch remaining edges (top edges) of trim to roof side edges.

9. Glue small shutters to front and back on both sides of each bird hole. Glue large shutters to both sides of windows on birdhouse sides. Making sure bottom edges are even, glue one snowman and one snow woman to front, back and each side. Place roof on cottage and secure with glue.

Napkin Holder

1. Cut plastic canvas according to graphs (pages 106 and 107), cutting two snowmen, two snow women and four snow children. Cut one 44-hole x 14-hole piece for holder bottom. Holder bottom will remain unstitched.

2. Following graphs through step 4, stitch and Overcast snow people, working uncoded areas with white Continental Stitches.

3. When background stitching is completed, work black Backstitches and French Knots.

4. Stitch napkin holder sides; Overcast top edges. Whipstitch long sides to short sides, then Whipstitch sides to unstitched bottom.

5. Using photo as a guide, making sure bottom edges are even, center and glue one snow child to each side; glue one snowman and one snow woman to each long side.

Magnets

1. Cut one of each snowman, snow woman and snow child from plastic canvas according to graphs.

2. Stitch and Overcast snow people following graphs, working uncoded areas with white Continental Stitches.

3. When background stitching is completed, work black Backstitches and French Knots.

4. Glue one magnetic strip to backside of each snow person. ❄

COLOR KEY

Plastic Canvas Yarn	Yards
■ Black #00	22
■ Burgundy #03	6
▨ Fern #23	9
▨ Royal #32	108
□ White #41	73
▨ Camel #43	2
■ Dark royal #48	15
■ Watermelon #55	7
▨ Bright orange #58	2
□ Bright blue #60	3
Uncoded areas are white #41 Continental Stitches	
✏ Black #00 Backstitch	
● Black #00 French Knot	

Color numbers given are for Uniek Needloft plastic canvas yarn.

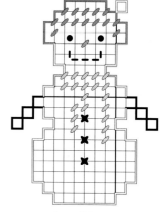

Snow Woman
14 holes x 19 holes
Cut 4 for birdhouse tissue topper
Cut 2 for napkin holder
Cut 1 for magnet

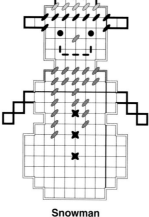

Snowman
14 holes x 20 holes
Cut 4 for birdhouse tissue topper
Cut 2 for napkin holder
Cut 1 for magnet

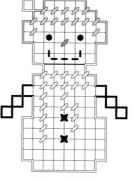

Snow Child
12 holes x 16 holes
Cut 4 for napkin holder
Cut 1 for magnet

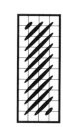

Large Shutter
4 holes x 10 holes
Cut 4

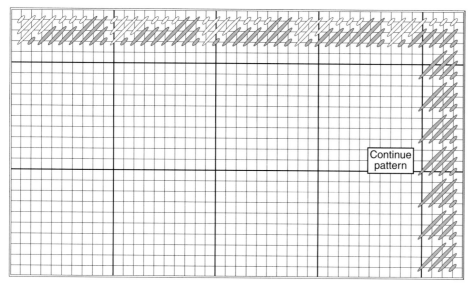

Napkin Holder Long Side
44 holes x 25 holes
Cut 2

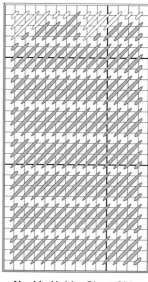

Napkin Holder Short Side
14 holes x 25 holes
Cut 2

106 *Let It Snow! in Plastic Canvas*

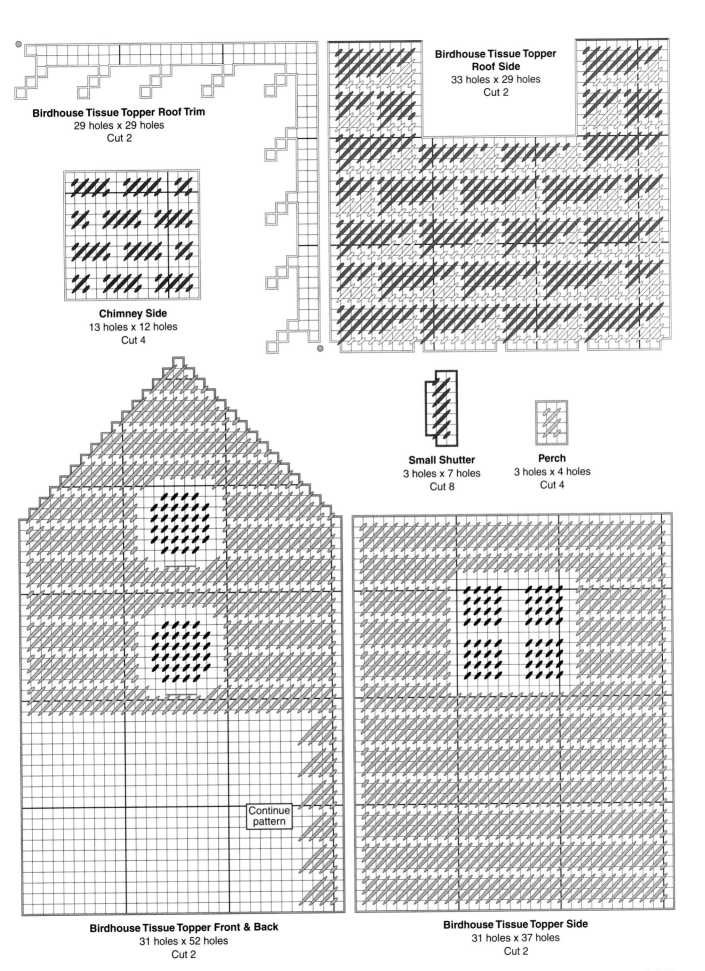

Birdhouse Tissue Topper Roof Trim
29 holes x 29 holes
Cut 2

Birdhouse Tissue Topper Roof Side
33 holes x 29 holes
Cut 2

Chimney Side
13 holes x 12 holes
Cut 4

Small Shutter
3 holes x 7 holes
Cut 8

Perch
3 holes x 4 holes
Cut 4

Continue
pattern

Birdhouse Tissue Topper Front & Back
31 holes x 52 holes
Cut 2

Birdhouse Tissue Topper Side
31 holes x 37 holes
Cut 2

Penguin Coaster

Design by Kathleen Hurley

 titch this jumbo coaster for using with a soup bowl or large café latte mug. It's sure to chase away those winter chills!

Skill Level

Beginner

Finished Size

6⅜ inches W x 7 inches H

Materials

- ½ sheet 7-count plastic canvas
- Coats & Clark Red Heart Classic worsted weight yarn Art. E267 as listed in color key
- #16 tapestry needle
- Hot-glue gun

Instructions

1. Cut plastic canvas according to graph.

2. Stitch and Overcast coaster following graph, working uncoded areas on penguin face and midsection with white Continental Stitches. For background, work two blue jewel stitches per hole.

3. When background stitching is completed, use a full strand white to work French Knots for falling snow. Use two plies yarn to work jockey red Backstitches for mouth and black French Knots for eyes. ✳

COLOR KEY

Worsted Weight Yarn	Yards
☐ White #1	6
■ Black #12	4
☐ Yellow #230	1
▨ Paddy green #686	2
▨ Forest green #689	2
▨ Grenadine #730	2
▨ Blue jewel #818	10
■ Jockey red #902	2
Uncoded areas on penguin are white #1 Continental Stitches	
╱ Jockey red #902 Backstitch	
○ White #1 French Knot	
● Black #12 French Knot	

Color numbers given are for Coats & Clark Red Heart Classic worsted weight yarn Art. E267.

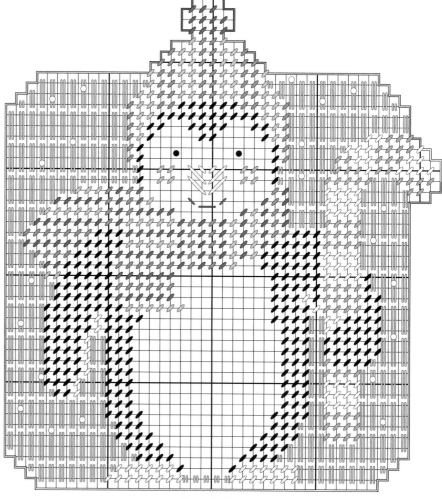

Penguin Coaster
42 holes x 46 holes
Cut 1

Snowflake Quilt-Block Set

Designs by Angie Arickx

Decorate your dining room in wintry blue with this stitched quilt-block set, including a place mat, napkin holder and trivet!

Skill Level

Beginner

Finished Size

Place mat: 16½ inches W x 13 inches H

Napkin holder: 6⅝ inches W x 3⅞ inches H x 2 inches D

Trivet: 7½ inches square

Materials

- 2 artist-size sheets Uniek QuickCount 7-count plastic canvas
- Uniek Needloft plastic canvas yarn as listed in color key
- #16 tapestry needle

Instructions

1. Cut plastic canvas according to graphs (this page and pages 111 and 112), making sure to cut the 109-hole x 85-hole place mat as one piece. Cut one 43-hole x 13-hole piece for napkin holder bottom that will remain unstitched.

2. Stitch pieces following graphs, working right half of place mat to center row of holes following graph. Turn graph and stitch left half from center row of holes until mat is completed.

3. Using royal throughout, Overcast place mat, trivet and top edges of napkin holder sides. Whipstitch holder long sides to holder short sides, then Whip-stitch sides to unstitched bottom. ❄

COLOR KEY	
Plastic Canvas Yarn	**Yards**
☐ Royal #32	98
☐ Silver #37	40
☐ White #41	40
■ Dark royal #48	34
Color numbers given are for Uniek Needloft plastic canvas yarn.	

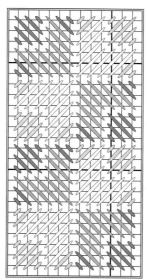

Napkin Holder Short Side
13 holes x 25 holes
Cut 2

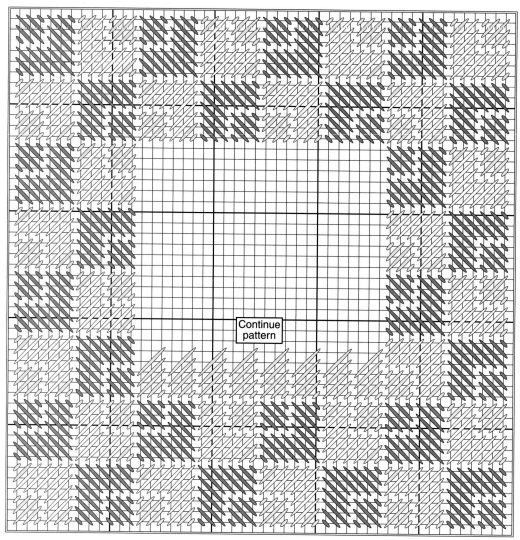

Trivet
49 holes x 49 holes
Cut 1

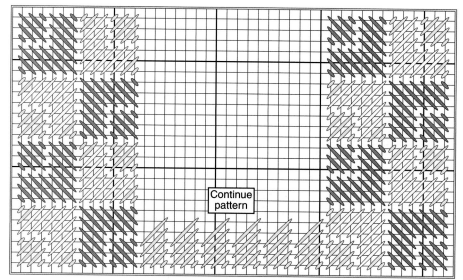

Napkin Holder Long Side
43 holes x 25 holes
Cut 2

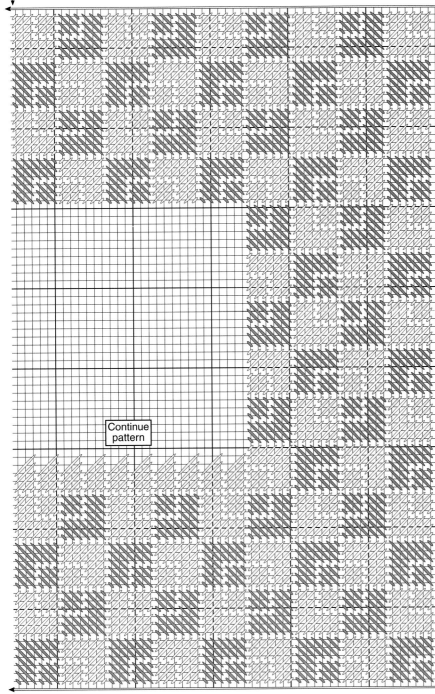

Continue
pattern

Snowflake Quilt Place Mat
109 holes x 85 holes
Cut 1
Stitch right half as graphed
Turn graph and continue
stitching left half until completed

COLOR KEY	
Plastic Canvas Yarn	**Yards**
☐ Royal #32	98
▨ Silver #37	40
☐ White #41	40
▨ Dark royal #48	34
Color numbers given are for Uniek Needloft plastic canvas yarn.	

Snowflake Shapes

Designs by Ruby Thacker

No two snowflakes are alike, and neither are these in this doily and gift-box set.

Skill Level

Intermediate

Finished Size

Doily: 14¼ inches x 13¾ inches

Boxes: 5⅝ inches x 4⅞ inches x 2¼ inches to 3⅛ inches H

Materials

- 1½ sheets Darice Ultra Stiff 7-count plastic canvas
- 13 (5-inch) Uniek QuickShape plastic canvas hexagons
- Uniek Needloft plastic canvas yarn as listed in color key
- Caron International Christmas Glitter worsted weight yarn Article 1285 as listed in color key
- #16 tapestry needle
- 6 (1½-inch) white tassels (optional)

Doily

1. Stitch six snowflake hexagons following snowflake graphs A–F (pages 116 and 117), using white plastic canvas yarn for snowflake motifs and royal for background color. Work doily center (page 117) entirely with royal stitches as graphed.

2. Following assembly diagram (page 116), place six snowflake hexagons around doily center. Using royal throughout, Whipstitch together; Overcast remaining edges.

Boxes

1. For royal box, cut six 17-hole-wide x 18-hole-high pieces for box sides and six 18-hole-wide x 5-hole-high pieces for lid sides. Cut box bottom from one plastic canvas hexagon following graph (page 117), cutting away gray areas. Box bottom will remain unstitched.

2. Continental Stitch box sides and lid sides with royal. For box top, choose one snowflake pattern from doily snowflakes and work snowflake motif on one hexagon with white Christmas glitter worsted weight yarn; fill in background on all segments with royal.

3. Using royal throughout, Whipstitch together 18-hole side edges of box sides, then Whipstitch box sides to unstitched box bottom, forming a six-sided box. Overcast top edges.

4. Whipstitch short edges of lid sides together, then Whipstitch to lid top. Overcast bottom edges.

5. For red box, repeat steps 1–4, using red box lid top and replacing royal with Christmas red.

6. For green box, repeat steps 1–4, cutting six 17-hole-wide x 13-hole-high pieces for box sides and replacing royal with Christmas green. *Note: 13-hole side edges of box sides will be Whipstitched together.*

7. *Optional:* Using photo as a guide, attach hangers of tassels to inside corners of one box lid. ❄

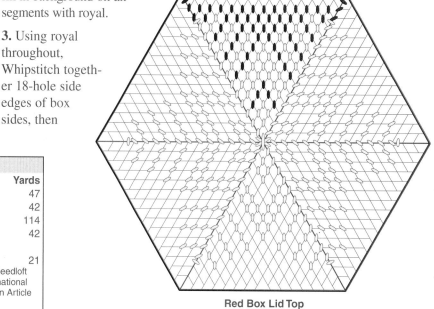

Red Box Lid Top
Stitch 1
Fill in all segments
with Christmas red pattern

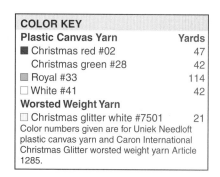

COLOR KEY	
Plastic Canvas Yarn	**Yards**
■ Christmas red #02	47
Christmas green #28	42
▨ Royal #33	114
☐ White #41	42
Worsted Weight Yarn	
☐ Christmas glitter white #7501	21
Color numbers given are for Uniek Needloft plastic canvas yarn and Caron International Christmas Glitter worsted weight yarn Article 1285.	

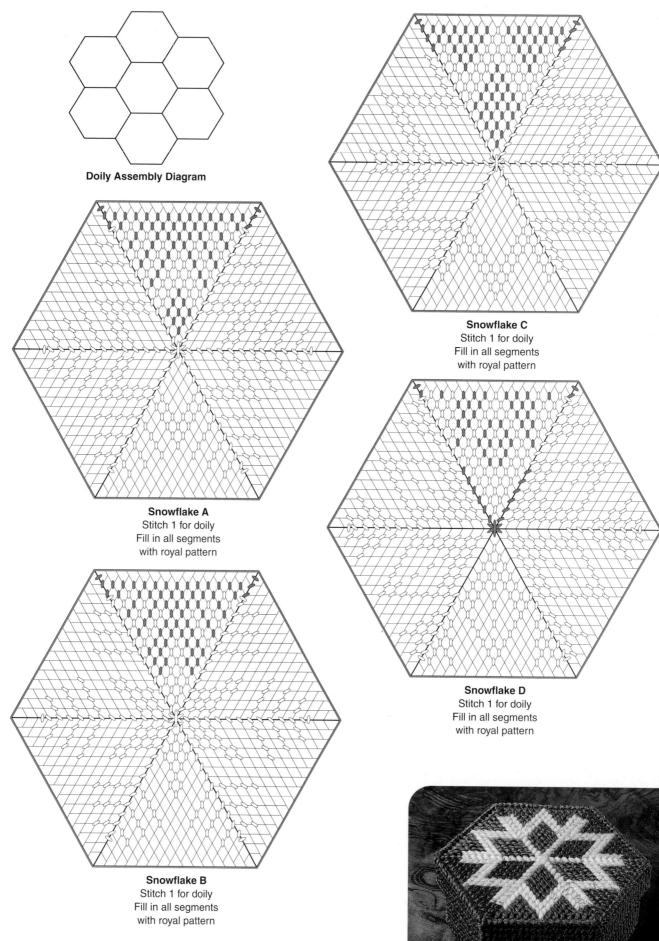

Doily Assembly Diagram

Snowflake A
Stitch 1 for doily
Fill in all segments
with royal pattern

Snowflake B
Stitch 1 for doily
Fill in all segments
with royal pattern

Snowflake C
Stitch 1 for doily
Fill in all segments
with royal pattern

Snowflake D
Stitch 1 for doily
Fill in all segments
with royal pattern

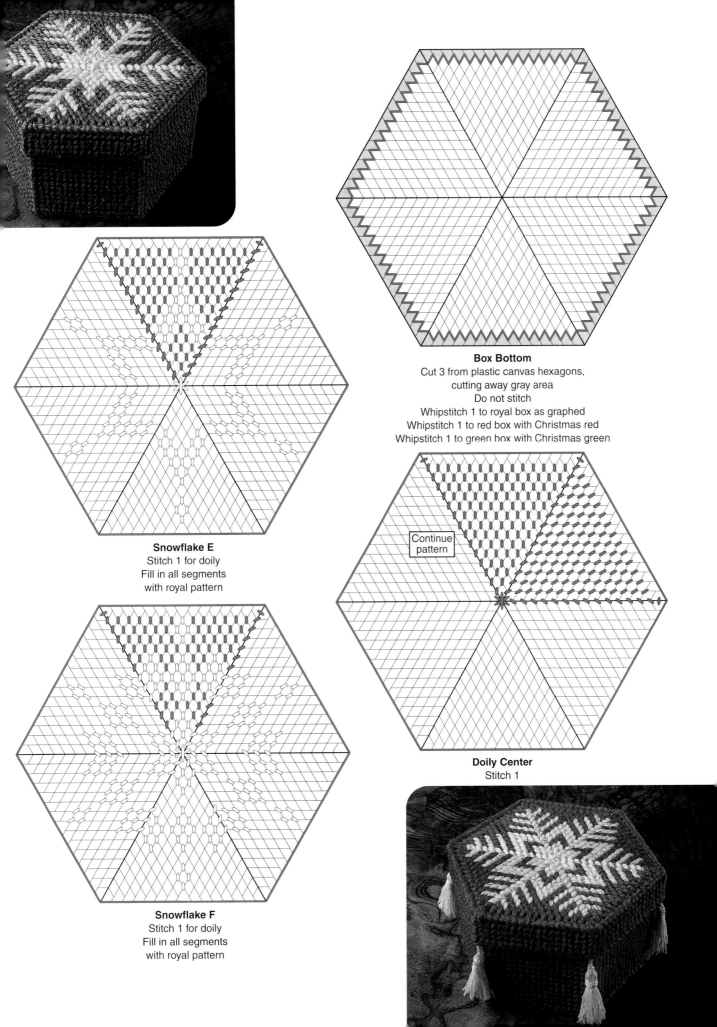

Box Bottom
Cut 3 from plastic canvas hexagons,
cutting away gray area
Do not stitch
Whipstitch 1 to royal box as graphed
Whipstitch 1 to red box with Christmas red
Whipstitch 1 to green box with Christmas green

Continue
pattern

Doily Center
Stitch 1

Snowflake E
Stitch 1 for doily
Fill in all segments
with royal pattern

Snowflake F
Stitch 1 for doily
Fill in all segments
with royal pattern

Snowy Trees & Snowman

Design by Joan Green

Surround a candle, bottle or jar with a hinged snow scene for a delightful wintry gift.

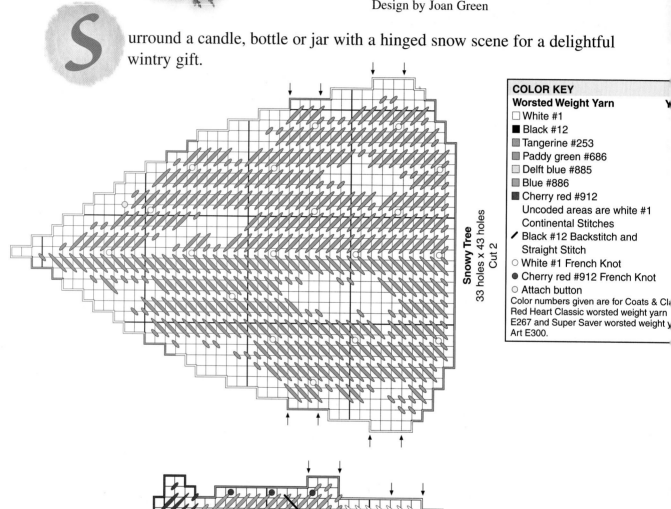

Snowy Tree
33 holes x 43 holes
Cut 2

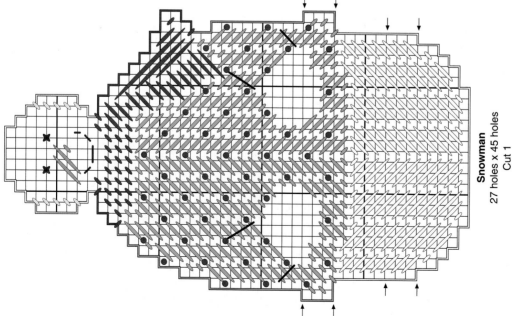

Snowman
27 holes x 45 holes
Cut 1

Skill Level

Beginner

Finished Size

4¼ inches W x 7⅛ inches H x 5 inches D

Materials

- ⅔ sheet Darice Ultra Stiff 7-count plastic canvas
- Coats & Clark Red Heart Classic worsted weight yarn Art. E267 as listed in color key
- Coats & Clark Red Heart Super Saver worsted weight yarn Art. E300 as listed in color key
- #16 tapestry needle
- 3½ inches red chenille stem
- 2 Mill Hill Products ceramic Red Bird buttons #86095 from Gay Bowles Sales Inc.
- Sewing needle and red sewing thread or 6-strand embroidery floss
- Fabric glue

Project Note

Candle should not be burned with this project; use candle for decoration only.

Instructions

1. Cut one snowman and two trees from plastic canvas according to graphs.

2. Stitch and Overcast pieces following graphs, working uncoded areas with white Continental Stitches and Overcasting the earmuff edges twice to accentuate.

3. When background stitching is completed, using 4 plies yarn, work sleeve outlines and mouth with black; work cherry red French Knots on jacket. Use 2 plies white to work French Knots on trees.

4. Working over the already Overcast edges throughout, Whipstitch trees together with white between bottom arrows along one side only. Whipstitch snowman to trees with white between bottom arrows and with blue between top arrows.

5. Using photo as a guide, bend red chenille stem to form headband of earmuffs, then glue ends to head behind earmuffs.

6. Using sewing needle and red sewing thread or embroidery floss, attach one red bird button to each tree where indicated on graph; knot ends and weave in to secure. *Note: Sample used left-facing red bird buttons. If using right-facing red bird buttons, attach to opposite side of trees.* ❈

Frosted Snowflakes

Design by Kathy Wirth

Stitch this elegant, white and silver candleholder for a sparkling centerpiece or festive accent for an end table. It is also perfect for a winter wedding!

Skill Level

Intermediate

Finished Size

5⅛ inches square x 4¼ inches H (holds 6-inch H x 2¾-inch-diameter pillar candle)

Materials

- 2 sheets Uniek QuickCount 7-count plastic canvas
- 4 (6-inch) Uniek QuickShape plastic canvas hearts
- 4 (6-inch) Uniek QuickShape plastic canvas hexagons
- ⅛-inch-wide Plastic Canvas 7 Metallic Needlepoint Yarn by Rainbow Gallery as listed in color key
- #16 tapestry needle
- ½ sheet white adhesive-backed Presto felt by Kunin Felt
- Nylon strapping tape

Project Notes

Candle should not be burned with this project; use candle for decoration only.

Make sure to keep metallic needlepoint yarn smooth and flat when stitching, Overcasting and Whipstitching.

When stitching base pieces, use small pieces of strapping tape to secure metallic yarn ends.

Instructions

1. Cut plastic canvas according to graphs, cutting away gray areas on plastic canvas hearts for candleholder sides and plastic canvas hexagons for snowflakes.

2. Trace base layer A on backing of felt sheet; cut 1/16-inch smaller than tracing all around. Also cut one 3⅜-inch square from felt.

3. Stitch holder sides and snowflakes following graphs, Overcasting silver points on snowflakes while stitching. Do not Overcast remaining edges of snowflakes. Overcast bottom edges of sides with white pearl.

4. Using silver through step 5, Overcast inside edges of holder sides, Whipstitching snowflakes to edges where indicated on graphs with green dots.

5. Whipstitch sides together, then Overcast around top edge of each side.

6. Place all three layer A pieces together, aligning edges. Work silver straight stitches through all three layers following graph.

7. Center all three layer B pieces on top of layer A and work silver stitches through all layers following layer B graph. Repeat with layers C and then D, stitching through additional layers each time.

8. Center sides on top of base layer D along blue lines; tack in place through all layers of base with white pearl at corners and centers of sides.

9. Remove paper backing from felt and apply larger square to bottom of base and smaller square to inside top of base. ❈

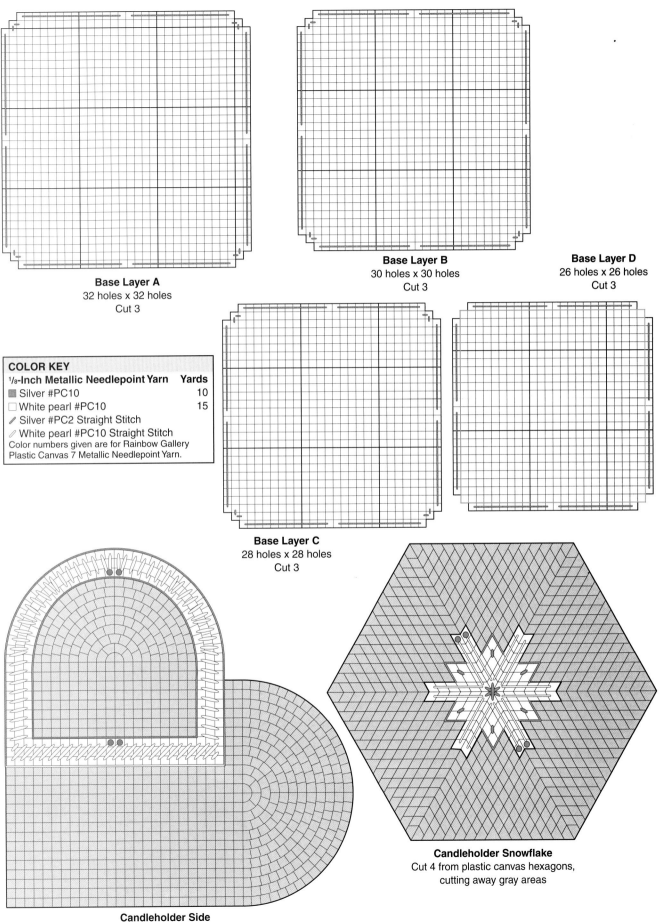

Base Layer A
32 holes x 32 holes
Cut 3

Base Layer B
30 holes x 30 holes
Cut 3

Base Layer D
26 holes x 26 holes
Cut 3

COLOR KEY

¹/₈-Inch Metallic Needlepoint Yarn	Yards
■ Silver #PC10	10
□ White pearl #PC10	15
⟋ Silver #PC2 Straight Stitch	
⟋ White pearl #PC10 Straight Stitch	

Color numbers given are for Rainbow Gallery
Plastic Canvas 7 Metallic Needlepoint Yarn.

Base Layer C
28 holes x 28 holes
Cut 3

Candleholder Snowflake
Cut 4 from plastic canvas hexagons,
cutting away gray areas

Candleholder Side
Cut 4 from plastic canvas hearts,
cutting away gray areas

Beaded Snowflakes

Designs by Joan Green

Bright white dimensional snowflake napkin rings add an elegant touch to your dining table when against a rich green or red linen napkin!

Skill Level

Beginner

Materials

Each napkin ring

- 2 (4-inch) squares 7-count plastic canvas
- Coats & Clark Red Heart Classic worsted weight yarn Art. E267 as listed in color key (see Project Notes)
- #16 tapestry needle
- 4 (4mm) silver beads from Designs by Joan Green
- Silver glitter stem from Designs by Joan Green
- Sewing needle and white sewing thread
- Fabric glue

Finished Size

Approximately 3½ inches x 3½ inches, excluding ring

Project Notes

Yardage given is for one snowflake. Each snowflake will take the same amount of yarn.

Two pieces are combined for each snowflake. Mix and match patterns, trying different combinations as desired. Samples used the following combinations: A and F, B and E, C and D, D and F.

Instructions

1. Cut plastic canvas according to graphs, cutting desired number of each snowflake.

2. Overcast snowflakes, working Continental Stitches as graphed in solid areas while Overcasting.

3. Hold desired two pieces together, so that points of top snowflake are between points of bottom snowflake. Using sewing needle and white sewing thread, attach silver beads to center of snowflake, working through both layers and pulling tightly. Knot and weave in ends to secure.

4. Make a circle with glitter stem, twisting ends together slightly. Poke each end through loop made by other end and twist tightly together. Flatten twisted side of circle a little and glue to wrong side of snowflake, forming napkin ring.

5. Repeat steps 3 and 4 for each snowflake. ❄

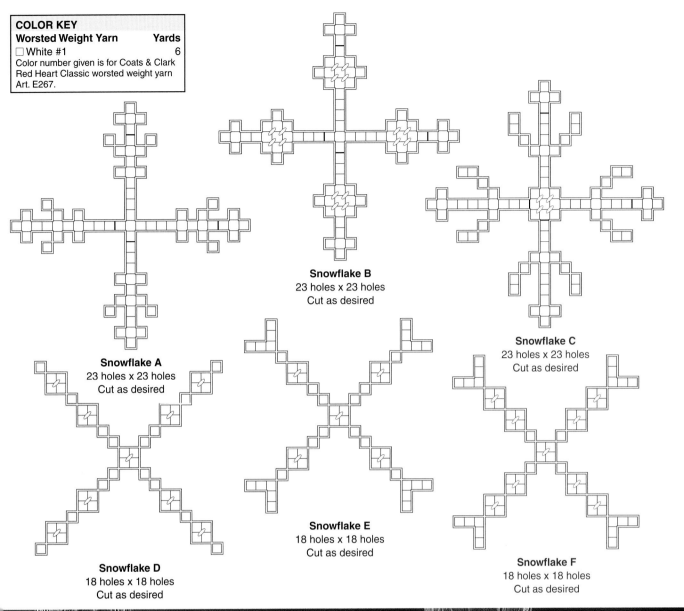

Snowflake B
23 holes x 23 holes
Cut as desired

Snowflake C
23 holes x 23 holes
Cut as desired

Snowflake A
23 holes x 23 holes
Cut as desired

Snowflake E
18 holes x 18 holes
Cut as desired

Snowflake F
18 holes x 18 holes
Cut as desired

Snowflake D
18 holes x 18 holes
Cut as desired

Winter Cardinals

Design by Kristine Loffredo

The cardinal, a winter favorite, dresses up tapered candles with simple elegance.

Skill Level

Beginner

Finished Size

Cardinal only: 4 inches W x 6½ inches H

Candle hug only: 2 inches H x 1¼ inches in diameter

Materials

- 1 sheet Uniek QuickCount stiff 7-count plastic canvas
- Uniek Needloft plastic canvas yarn as listed in color key
- Uniek metallic craft cord as listed in color key
- #16 tapestry needle
- Hot-glue gun

Project Note

Do not leave burning candles unattended.

Instructions

1. Cut plastic canvas according to graphs.

2. Stitch cardinals and wings following graphs, reversing one cardinal and one wing before stitching and reversing direction of stitches on these pieces. Do not stitch area indicated with blue line on cardinals at this time.

3. When background stitching is completed, work brown Backstitches on cardinals, outlining eyes. Overcast cardinals following graph.

4. Using red throughout, Overcast wings, leaving top edge of each unworked. Whipstitch top edge of wing to bar indicated with blue line on corresponding cardinal.

5. For each candle hug, Overlap short ends where indicated and stitch following graph. Overcast edges.

6. Glue overlapped area of one hug to backside of one cardinal. Repeat with remaining cardinal and hug. ❋

COLOR KEY

Plastic Canvas Yarn	Yards
■ Red #01	7
☐ Lemon #20	1
■ Black #00 Overcasting	1
■ Brown #15 Backstitch	1
▨ Camel #43 Overcasting	1
Metallic Craft Cord	
☐ Gold #55001	4

Color numbers given are for Uniek Needloft plastic canvas yarn and metallic craft cord.

Overlap

Winter Cardinal
19 holes x 41 holes
Cut 2, reverse 1,
reversing direction of stitches

Overlap

Candle Hug
25 holes x 25 holes
Cut 2

Winter Cardinal Wing
22 holes x 15 holes
Cut 2, reverse 1,
reversing direction of stitches

Snowy Cardinal

Design by Nancy Dorman

Stitch a vibrant, red cardinal topper to transform an ordinary tissue box into a wonderful winter display!

Skill Level
Beginner

Finished Size
Fits boutique-style tissue box

Materials
- 1½ sheets 7-count plastic canvas
- Worsted weight yarn as listed in color key
- 6-strand embroidery floss as listed in color key
- #16 tapestry needle

Instructions

1. Cut plastic canvas according to graphs.

2. Stitch pieces following graphs, working uncoded areas with light gray Continental Stitches.

3. When background stitching is completed, work forest green Straight Stitches for pine needles on branches and white French Knots for falling snow. Work Backstitches around eye with medium yellow floss.

4. Using forest green throughout, Overcast bottom edges of sides and inside edges on top. Whipstitch sides together, then Whipstitch sides to top with a Binding Stitch, beginning with steps A–D, then continuing with steps C and D. ❊

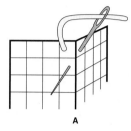

A

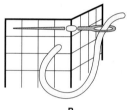

B

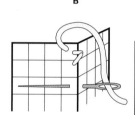

C

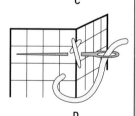

D

Binding Stitch

COLOR KEY	
Worsted Weight Yarn	**Yards**
■ Forest green	45
■ Red	10
■ Burgundy	8
□ White	5
■ Medium brown	5
▨ Light taupe	2
■ Black	2
Uncoded areas are light gray Continental Stitches	28
╱ Forest green Straight Stitch	
○ White French Knot	
6-Strand Embroidery Floss	
╱ Medium yellow Backstitch	1

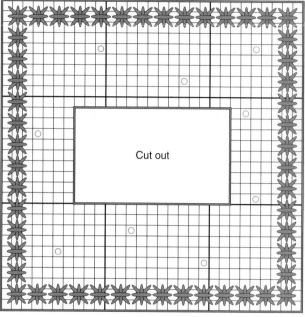

Snowy Cardinal Top
29 holes x 29 holes
Cut 1

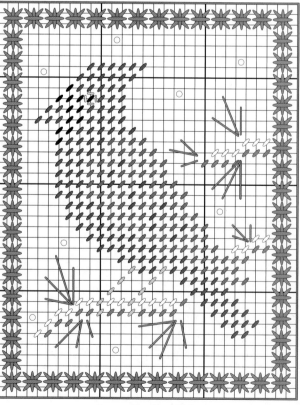

Snowy Cardinal Side
29 holes x 37 holes
Cut 4

Snow Cat Angels

Designs by Joan Green

Delight the cat lover in your life with this kitty duo accented in gold metallic yarn.

COLOR KEY

Worsted Weight Yarn	Yards
■ Black #12	2
□ Light teal #335	65
▨ Medium teal #359	34
■ Skipper blue #848	34
╱ Black #12 Backstitch	
● Black #12 French Knot	

Furry Yarn and Wispy Fringe
Uncoded areas are ermine (white)
#FF1 and white #AR2 — **20 each**
╱ Ermine (white) #FF1 and
white #AR2 Overcasting

⅛-Inch Metallic Needlepoint Yarn
╱ Gold #PC1 Overcasting and
Whipstitching — **8**

¹⁄₁₆-Inch Metallic Needlepoint Yarn
○ Gold #PM51 French Knot — **1**

Color numbers given are for Coats & Clark Red Heart Classic worsted weight yarn Art. E267 and Rainbow Gallery Faux Fur very furry singles yarn, Arctic Rays Wispy Fringe and Plastic Canvas 7 and Plastic Canvas 10 Metallic Needlepoint Yarn.

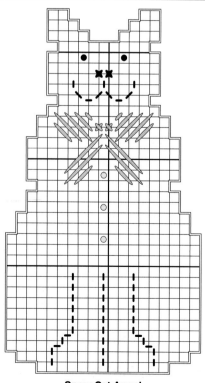

Snow Cat Angel
19 holes x 34 holes
Cut 1

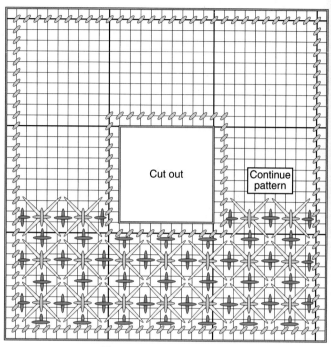

Tissue Box Cover Top
31 holes x 31 holes
Cut 1

Cut out

Continue pattern

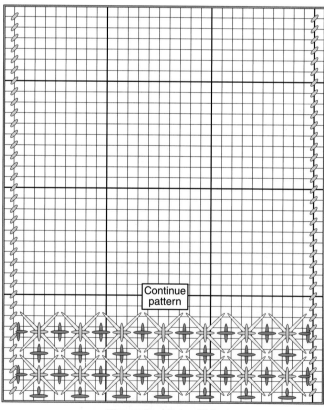

Continue pattern

Tissue Box Cover Side
31 holes x 37 holes
Cut 4

Skill Level
Beginner

Finished Size
Cat angel: 3¾ inches W x 5¼ inches H, excluding hanger

Tissue box cover: Fits boutique-style tissue box

Materials
- 1½ sheets 7-count plastic canvas
- Coats & Clark Red Heart Classic worsted weight yarn Art. E267 as listed in color key
- Faux Fur very furry singles yarn by Rainbow Gallery as listed in color key
- Arctic Rays Wispy Fringe by Rainbow Gallery as listed in color key
- ⅛-inch-wide Plastic Canvas 7 Metallic Needlepoint Yarn by Rainbow Gallery as listed in color key
- 1⁄16-inch-wide Plastic Canvas 10 Metallic Needlepoint Yarn by Rainbow Gallery as listed in color key
- #16 tapestry needle
- 2 (3¾-inch) gold puffy angel wings from Designs by Joan Green
- Gold glitter stem from Designs by Joan Green
- Fabric glue

Instructions
1. Cut plastic canvas according to graphs.

2. For tissue box cover, Continental Stitch borders where indicated with a single strand (4 plies) medium teal first, then work large Cross Stitches with a double strand (8 plies) light teal yarn.

3. Using single strand yarn throughout, work skipper blue Upright Cross Stitches between large Cross Stitches, filling in as indicated at sides, top and bottom. Using medium teal, work Upright Cross Stitches over intersections of large Cross Stitches.

4. Using gold ⅛-inch metallic

needlepoint yarn throughout, Overcast bottom edges of sides and inside edges of top. Whipstitch sides together, then Whipstitch sides to top.

5. Stitch cats following graph, working uncoded areas with Continental Stitches, combining one strand ermine furry yarn and one strand white wispy fringe. Cross Stitch noses with 2 plies black.

6. When background stitching is completed, use 2 plies black to work French Knots for eyes and Backstitches for mouth and legs. Work gold 1⁄16-inch gold metallic

needlepoint yarn French Knots for buttons.

7. Use photo as a guide through step 9. For each cat, cut a 5-inch length of gold glitter stem. Bend one end into a halo; glue to top center back of cat's head.

8. Glue puffy gold wings to back of cats. Center and glue one angel to one side of tissue box cover.

9. For hanger, cut an 8-inch length 1⁄16-inch gold metallic needlepoint yarn. Glue ends to top backside of remaining angel. ✳

Sitting Snowman

Design by Nancy Marshall

 his cute snowman is designed to hold your favorite small candle, while hanging his legs over the edge of a shelf.

Skill Level

Intermediate

Finished Size

3½ inches W x 11½ inches H x 3⅜ inches D (sits 7¾ inches tall)

Materials

- ¾ sheet clear 7-count plastic canvas
- ½ sheet white 7-count plastic canvas
- Uniek Needloft plastic canvas yarn as listed in color key
- 6-strand embroidery floss as listed in color key
- #16 tapestry needle
- 2 (6mm) round black beads
- ½-inch flat green button
- ¾-inch length orange chenille stem
- ½ yard ⁷⁄₁₆-inch wide red and green plaid ribbon
- Sewing needle
- Black and white sewing thread
- Transparent nylon thread
- Glass votive candle holder
- Red votive candle
- Hot-glue gun

Project Note

Candle should not be burned with this project; use candle for decoration only.

Cutting & Stitching

1. For backing, cut one body following graph, one 18-hole x 18-hole piece for snowman's lap and one 18-hole x 23-hole piece for lower legs from white plastic canvas. Backing pieces will remain unstitched.

2. Using white yarn, Whipstitch backing pieces together along 18-hole edges in the following order: body, lap, lower legs. Set aside.

3. From clear plastic canvas, cut pieces according to graphs (this page and page 133). Also cut one 18-hole x 18-hole piece for lap and stitch with white Continental Stitches.

4. Stitch remaining pieces following graphs, reversing two arms before stitching and working uncoded areas with white Continental Stitches.

5. When background stitching is completed, Backstitch mouth with red floss. Overcast hat brim and boot toes following graphs.

COLOR KEY

Plastic Canvas Yarn	Yards
■ Black #00	10
□ Pink #07	1
■ Holly #27	9
▨ Gray #38	1
Uncoded areas are white #41 Continental Stitches	40
⁄ White #41 Whipstitching	
6-Strand Embroidery Floss	
⁄ Red Backstitch	1
● Attach black bead	
● Attach green button	

Color numbers given are for Uniek Needloft plastic canvas yarn.

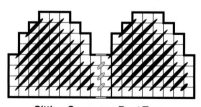

Sitting Snowman Boot Toes
18 holes x 8 holes
Cut 1 from clear

Sitting Snowman Inner Mitten
8 holes x 8 holes
Cut 2 from clear

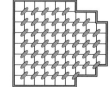

Sitting Snowman Outer Mitten
9 holes x 8 holes
Cut 2 from clear

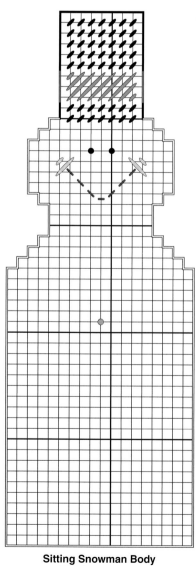

Sitting Snowman Body
18 holes x 50 holes
Cut 1 from clear
Stitch as graphed
Cut 1 from white for backing
Do not stitch

6. Using sewing needle and black sewing thread, attach black beads for eyes where indicated on graph. Using sewing needle and white sewing thread, attach green button to body where indicated on graph. Using photo as a guide, glue orange chenille stem to face for nose.

Assembly

1. For snowman front, following graphs, Whipstitch stitched body, lap and lower legs together in same order as in step 2 under cutting and stitching.

2. Beginning at hat and using adjacent colors, Whipstitch backing to snowman front along top, side and bottom edges. *Note: Because lower legs backing is one hole shorter than stitched lower legs, snowman will bend at legs as pieces are joined.*

3. Using photo as a guide through step 8, center and glue hat brim to bottom of hat and top of face. Glue boot toes to bottom of lower legs, making sure bottom edges are even.

4. Using green throughout, for outer arms, Whipstitch one outer mitten each to cuffs of one left arm and one right arm. For inner arms, Whipstitch inner mittens to cuffs of remaining two arm pieces.

5. Matching edges and beginning at mittens, Whipstitch two assembled inner and outer arm and mitten pieces together with adjacent colors. *Note: Because inner mittens are one hole shorter than outer mittens, arm will bend at wrist.* Repeat with remaining arm.

6. Place arms on snowman so that bend at wrists are on front corners of lap. Using transparent thread, sew mittens to lap along outside edges of lap and at knees; sew finger edges together at center.

7. Bring body up to a 90-degree angle and glue arms to edges of body so that about one row of holes extends beyond body edge.

8. Tie scarf around neck; trim and glue ends to body, out of candle flame's reach.

9. Place holder with candle in snowman's lap. ✳

Graphs continued on page 133

Mini Candy Cup

Design by Kathleen Hurley

Tuck sweets or tiny treasures into this friendly snowman candy cup! Filled with goodies, it makes a wonderful party favor!

Skill Level
Beginner

Finished Size
4¼ inches W x 6½ inches H x 2¾ inches D

Materials
- ½ sheet 7-count plastic canvas
- Coats & Clark Red Heart Classic worsted weight yarn Art. E267 as listed in color key
- #16 tapestry needle
- Hot-glue gun

Instructions

1. Cut plastic canvas according to graphs. Cup bottom will remain unstitched.

2. Stitch and Overcast snowman and arms following graphs, working uncoded areas with white Continental Stitches and reversing one arm before stitching.

3. When background stitching is completed, use 2 plies yarn to work Backstitches, Cross Stitches and French Knots on snowman face and vest.

4. Stitch cup side following graph, overlapping two holes of short sides as indicated on graph before stitching. Overcast top edge; Whipstitch bottom edge to unstitched bottom.

5. Using photo as a guide, glue or tack arms to snowman at shoulders. Center and glue candy cup to snowman, making sure bottom edges are even. ❄

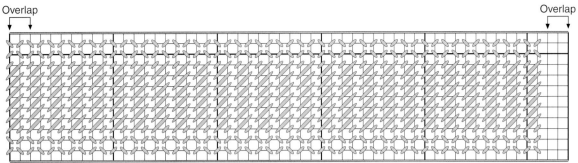

Candy Cup Side
54 holes x 12 holes
Cut 1

Overlap

Overlap

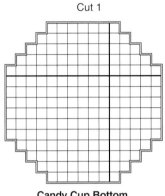

Candy Cup Bottom
15 holes x 15 holes
Cut 1
Do not stitch

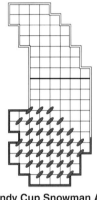

Candy Cup Snowman Arm
8 holes x 17 holes
Cut 2, reverse 1

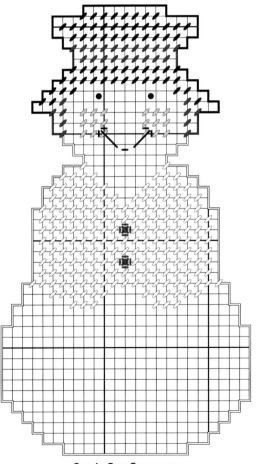

Candy Cup Snowman
24 holes x 42 holes
Cut 1

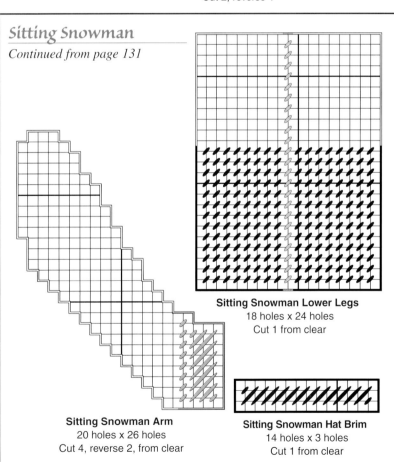

Sitting Snowman
Continued from page 131

Sitting Snowman Lower Legs
18 holes x 24 holes
Cut 1 from clear

Sitting Snowman Arm
20 holes x 26 holes
Cut 4, reverse 2, from clear

Sitting Snowman Hat Brim
14 holes x 3 holes
Cut 1 from clear

Snowy Lodge Coaster Set

Designs by Joan Green

ive your living room the atmosphere of a cozy lodge in the woods with this coaster set designed in warm, country colors.

Finished Size

Coasters: 3⅜ inches square

Coaster box: 4 inches square x 1⅜ inches H

Materials

- 1 sheet 7-count plastic canvas
- Coats & Clark Red Heart Classic worsted weight yarn Art. E267 as listed in color key
- Coats & Clark Red Heart Super Saver worsted weight yarn Art. E300 as listed in color key
- #16 tapestry needle
- Cashmere tan adhesive-backed Presto felt by Kunin Felt (optional)

Skill Level

Beginner

Instructions

1. Cut plastic canvas according to graphs. Also cut one 24-hole x 24-hole piece for box bottom. Box bottom will remain unstitched.

2. Stitch pieces following graphs, working uncoded areas on snowflake coasters and lid top with Windsor blue Continental Stitches and uncoded areas on tree coasters with country blue Continental Stitches.

3. When background stitching is completed, using 4 plies yarn, work forest green Straight Stitches for pine needles on tree coasters and white Straight

Stitches on snowflake coasters.

4. Using 4 plies white, work French Knots on snowflake coasters. Using 2 plies white, work French Knots on lid top and tree coasters for falling snow.

5. Overcast snowflake coasters with country blue.

6. Using Windsor blue throughout, Overcast tree coasters, top edges of box sides and bottom edges of lid sides. Whipstitch box sides together, then Whipstitch box sides to unstitched box bottom. Whipstitch lid sides together, then Whipstitch lid sides to lid top.

7. *Optional:* Cut two pieces cashmere tan felt slightly smaller than box bottom, then apply to both sides of box bottom. ❋

COLOR KEY	
Worsted Weight Yarn	**Yards**
☐ White #1	3
▨ Linen #330	14
▨ Forest green #689	3
▨ Country blue #882	15
■ Cardinal #917	13
Uncoded areas on lid top and snowflake coasters are Windsor blue #380 Continental Stitches	20
Uncoded areas on tree coasters are country blue #882 Continental Stitches	
╱ Windsor blue #380 Overcasting and Whipstitching	
╱ White #1 Straight Stitch	
╱ Forest green #689 Straight Stitch	
○ White #1 (2-ply) French Knot	
○ White #1 (4-ply) French Knot	
Color numbers given are for Coats & Clark Red Heart Classic worsted weight yarn Art. E267 and Super Saver worsted weight yarn Art. E300.	

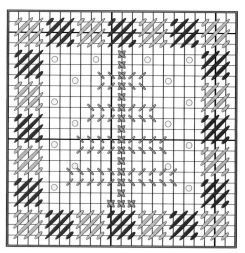

Tree Coaster
22 holes x 22 holes
Cut 2

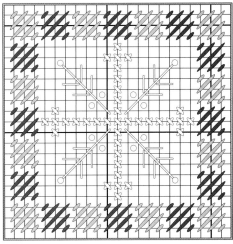

Snowflake Coaster
22 holes x 22 holes
Cut 2

Coaster Box Side
24 holes x 7 holes
Cut 4

Lid Side
25 holes x 3 holes
Cut 4

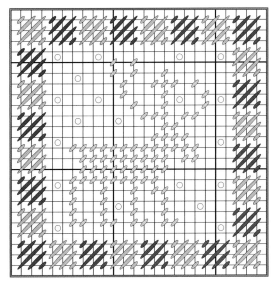

Lid Top
25 holes x 25 holes
Cut 1

Tabletop Decor **135**

Christmas Joy

You're never too old to wish for a white Christmas! This collection of 34 festive, merry Christmas gifts and decorations will add stitching pleasure to the winter months and holiday season!

Holly Basket

Design by Janna Britton

T uck an assortment of delicious Christmas treats into this vibrant basket for sharing with co-workers!

Skill Level

Beginner

Finished Size

Lid only: 9½ inches W x 15½ inches L

Materials

- 1 (12-inch x 18-inch) sheet Uniek QuickCount stiff 7-count plastic canvas
- Uniek Needloft plastic canvas yarn as listed in color key
- Uniek Needloft metallic craft cord as listed in color key
- #16 tapestry needle
- 15-inch x 10-inch x 6-inch willow basket, excluding handle (opening on basket is approximately 8 inches wide x 13 inches long)
- 10-inch x 15-inch light iron-on fusible sheet
- 10-inch x 15-inch white fabric (for lining)
- 18 (¼-inch) red pompoms
- 3 (12mm) red jingle bells
- 2 (4-inch) lengths red chenille stem
- 1 yard ⅛-inch-wide white satin ribbon
- 2 yards 1½-inch coordinating wire-edged ribbon
- Low-temperature glue gun

Cutting & Stitching

1. Cut plastic canvas according to graphs (pages 139 and 140).

2. Following manufacturer's directions, adhere fusible sheet to fabric. Using plastic canvas lid pieces as templates, cut fabric slightly smaller all around; set aside.

3. Following graphs through step 5, Stitch and Overcast holly leaves A, B and C.

4. Stitch holly leaf outlines and veins on lid sides with holly yarn Continental Stitches. Fill in leaf centers with Christmas green and fern Slanted Gobelin Stitches.

5. Stitch plaid lines on lid sides and center strip in gold and Christmas red, then work remaining uncoded areas with white Continental Stitches.

Assembly

1. Following graphs and using white throughout, Whipstitch center strip to long edge of each side piece, centering strip between sides and matching plaid lines. Overcast remaining edges.

2. Following manufacturer's directions, adhere fabric with fusible sheet to wrong sides of lid pieces.

3. Using photo as a guide through step 6, cut ⅛-inch-wide white ribbon in half. On each side of assembled lid, wrap one length around outside of handle, then thread ends from top to bottom through holes indicated on sides. Tie in a knot on inside of basket under lid.

4. With 1½-inch-wide coordinating ribbon, make a multi-loop bow with 9- to 10-inch tails. Wrap one red chenille stem around center and twist tightly to secure. Center and glue bow to center strip. Arrange loops and tails as desired, trimming tails in a "V"; lightly glue tails in place.

5. Glue pompoms in clusters of three to lid sides where indicated on graph with red dots.

6. Insert remaining red chenille stem through jingle bells. Twist end closed; glue chenille stem to back of leaf B at one tip. Glue leaves under handle on one side of basket, placing leaf B in the center with bells at top. ✳

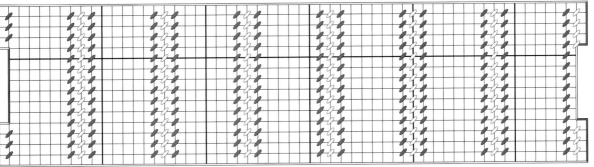

Holly Basket Lid Center
57 holes x 15 holes
Cut 1

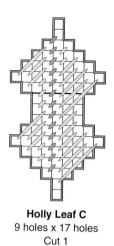

Holly Leaf C
9 holes x 17 holes
Cut 1

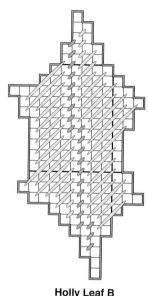

Holly Leaf B
13 holes x 25 holes
Cut 1

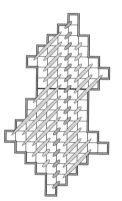

Holly Leaf A
10 holes x 17 holes
Cut 1

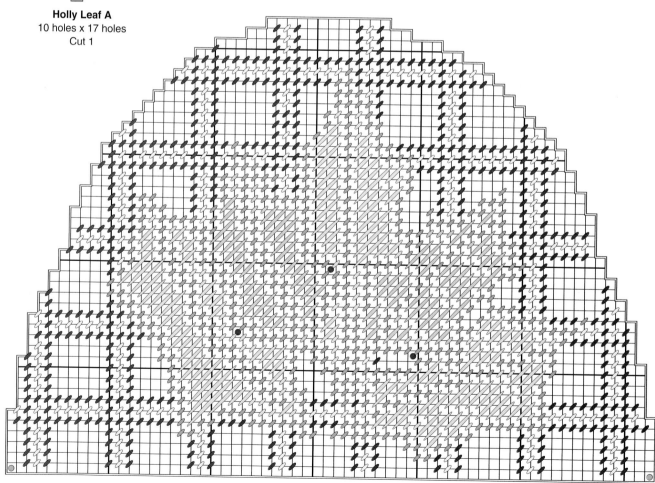

Holly Basket Lid Side
63 holes x 43 holes
Cut 2

140 *Let It Snow! in Plastic Canvas*

Christmas Glass Cozies

Designs by Vickery Designs

Subtle shades of red and green add beautiful detail to this pair of handsome holiday glass covers!

Finished Size

Poinsettia Cozy: 4¼ inches H x 3½ inches in diameter

Holly & Berries Cozy: 3¾ inches H x 3½ inches in diameter

Materials

- 1 sheet 7-count plastic canvas
- 2 (4-inch) Uniek QuickShape plastic canvas radial circles
- Uniek Needloft plastic canvas yarn as listed in color key
- Uniek Needloft metallic craft cord as listed in color key
- #16 tapestry needle

Skill Level

Beginner

Instructions

1. For each cozy bottom, cut the two most outer rows of holes from one plastic canvas radial circle. Cut cozy sides from plastic canvas according to graphs (page 142).

2. Stitch cozy sides, working uncoded areas with white Continental Stitches and overlapping one hole as indicated before stitching.

3. For each cozy, using white,

Overcast top edge of side, then Whipstitch bottom edge to bottom. ✳

COLOR KEY	
Plastic Canvas Yarn	**Yards**
■ Red #01	8
■ Christmas red #01	5
☐ Fern #23	9
■ Holly #27	9
■ Forest #29	6
☐ Watermelon #55	5
Uncoded areas are white #41 Continental Stitches	37
✎ White #41 Overcasting and Whipstitching	
Metallic Craft Cord	
■ White/gold #55007	6
Color numbers given are for Uniek Needloft plastic canvas yarn and metallic craft cord.	

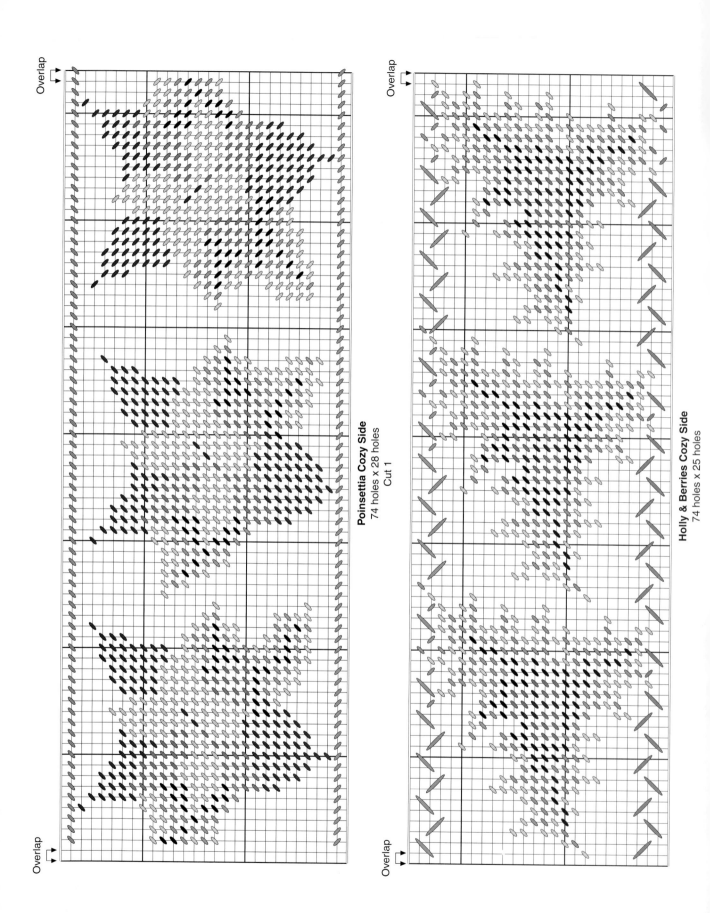

Poinsettia Cozy Side
74 holes x 28 holes
Cut 1

Holly & Berries Cozy Side
74 holes x 25 holes

Overlap

Overlap

Christmas Home Tissue Topper

Design by Angie Arickx

Two festive scenes adorn the sides of this tissue box cover. A decorated tree with gifts and fireplace mantel will remind you of your home for the holidays!

Skill Level

Beginner

Finished Size

Fits boutique-style tissue box

Materials

- 1 artist-size sheet Uniek QuickCount 7-count plastic canvas
- Uniek Needloft plastic canvas yarn as listed in color key
- #16 tapestry needle
- Hot-glue gun

Instructions

1. Cut plastic canvas according to graphs (pages 144 and 145).

2. Stitch hearth and topper pieces following graphs, working uncoded areas with camel Continental Stitches.

3. Using camel through step 4, Overcast inside edges of top and inside edges of fireplace sides. For hearth, Overcast all outside edges and inside edges from dot to dot on two sides.

4. Whipstitch sides together then Whipstitch sides to top. Place topper inside hearth opening, aligning opening on fireplace sides with Overcast edges, then Whipstitch sides to hearth.

5. Stitch and Overcast remaining pieces following graphs, working uncoded areas on fireplace inserts with brown Continental Stitches.

6. When background stitching is completed, work Christmas red French Knots on Christmas tree.

7. Using photo as a guide, center and glue fireplace inserts in place behind openings on sides, then glue one mantelpiece, one wreath and four stockings in place to each side above opening. Glue one Christmas tree, one star and two gifts to each remaining side. ❄

COLOR KEY

Plastic Canvas Yarn

		Yards
▲	Black #00	1
◢	Christmas red #02	14
▽	Tangerine #11	1
◢	Maple #13	4
◢	Cinnamon #14	7
◢	Gold #17	2
◢	Holly #27	14
◢	Eggshell #39	26
◢	Beige #40	39
◢	White #41	10

Uncoded areas on fireplace inserts are brown #15 Continental Stitches

	Uncoded areas on hearth and topper pieces are camel #43 Continental Stitches	40
◢	Camel #43 Overcasting and Whipstitching	
●	Christmas red #02 French Knot	

Color numbers given are for Uniek Needloft plastic canvas yarn.

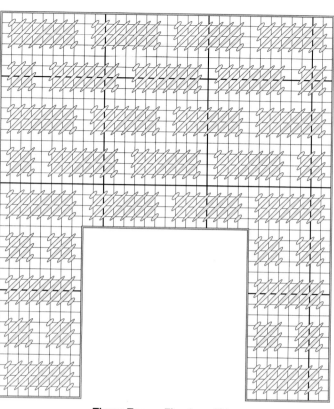

Tissue Topper Fireplace Side
32 holes x 36 holes
Cut 2

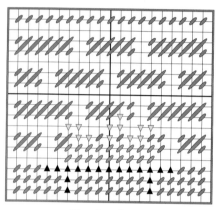

Fireplace Insert
20 holes x 18 holes
Cut 2

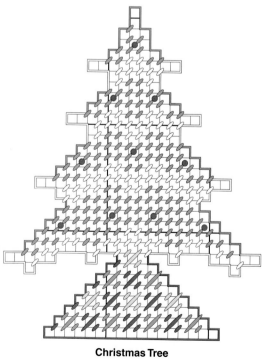

Christmas Tree
25 holes x 31 holes
Cut 2

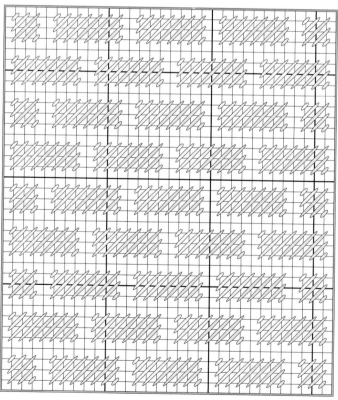

Tissue Topper Tree Side
32 holes x 36 holes
Cut 2

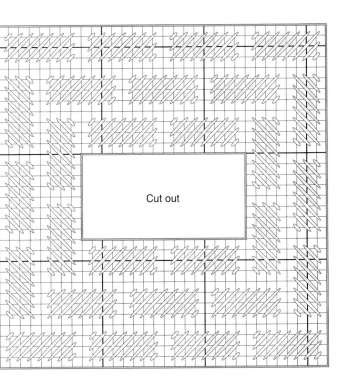

Tissue Topper Top
32 holes x 32 holes
Cut 1

Wreath
13 holes x 11 holes
Cut 2

Star
5 holes x 4 holes
Cut 2

Gift
7 holes x 5 holes
Cut 4

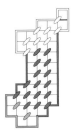

Stocking
6 holes x 11 holes
Cut 8

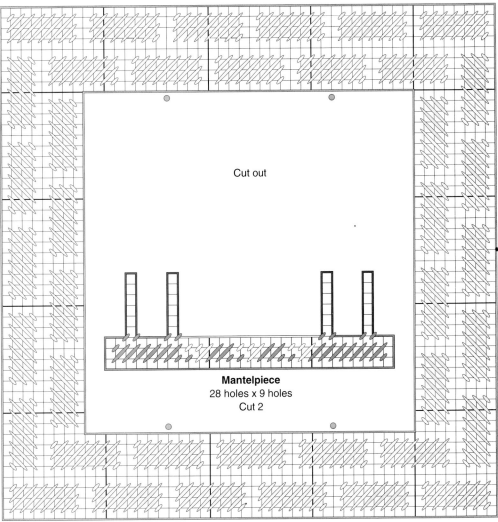

Mantelpiece
28 holes x 9 holes
Cut 2

Tissue Topper Hearth
48 holes x 48 holes
Cut 1

Mitten Garland

Design by Carol Krob

 tring these sparkling garlands across a doorway to wish "Happy Holidays!" to all who enter!

Skill Level

Beginner

Finished Size

Each mitten: 2⅜ inches W x 3⅝ inches H

Happy garland: approximate length when hung is 20 inches

Holidays garland: approximate length when hung is 25 inches

Materials

- 1¼ sheets 10-count plastic canvas
- DMC #3 pearl cotton as listed in color key
- Kreinik ⅛-inch Ribbon as listed in color key
- 14 (1-inch) tiny spring clothes-pins from Forster Inc.
- #20 tapestry needle
- Gold cord, braid or narrow ribbon
- Red, green or white adhesive-backed Presto felt by Kunin Felt (optional)

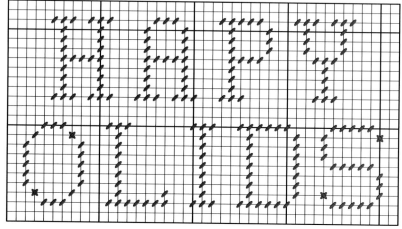

Mitten Garland Letters
Stitch with red or
very dark emerald green

Instructions

1. Cut plastic canvas according to graphs.

2. Following graphs through step 4, stitch and Overcast ornamental mitten, working uncoded area with very dark emerald green Continental Stitches.

3. Leaving uncoded areas in centers unworked at this time, stitch and Overcast letter mittens, working seven as graphed and six reversing red and green areas.

4. Center and stitch letters in uncoded area of mittens, filling in with white Continental Stitches. Work red letters on mittens with green thumbs and green letters on mittens with red thumbs, beginning each word with a red letter, then working every other letter in the alternating color.

5. If desired, cut felt slightly smaller all around than each mitten, then attach to backside.

6. Attach mittens to gold cord, braid or ribbon with clothespins. If using one garland, place ornamental mitten between words. If using two garlands, one for each word, place ornamental mitten on the first garland at the end of the word "HAPPY." ✳

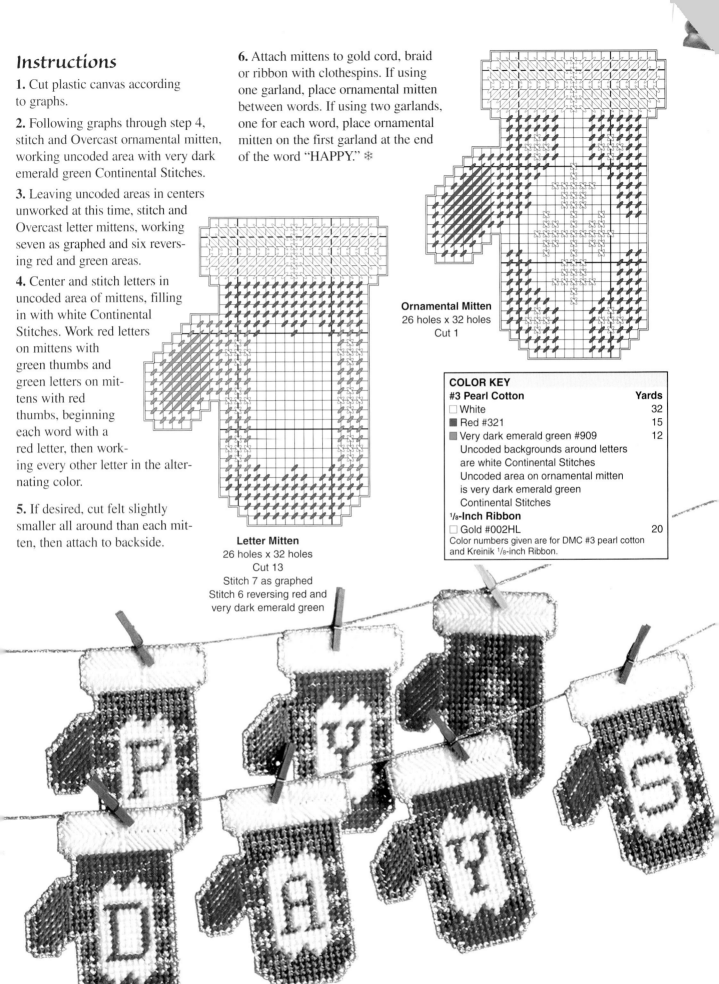

Ornamental Mitten
26 holes x 32 holes
Cut 1

Letter Mitten
26 holes x 32 holes
Cut 13
Stitch 7 as graphed
Stitch 6 reversing red and
very dark emerald green

COLOR KEY

#3 Pearl Cotton	Yards
☐ White	32
■ Red #321	15
▨ Very dark emerald green #909	12

Uncoded backgrounds around letters
are white Continental Stitches
Uncoded area on ornamental mitten
is very dark emerald green
Continental Stitches

⅛-Inch Ribbon

☐ Gold #002HL	20

Color numbers given are for DMC #3 pearl cotton
and Kreinik ⅛-inch Ribbon.

Santa's Coming Stocking

Design by Kathleen Hurley

Back this bright stocking with colorful felt and fill it with all sorts of small gifts and yummy treats!

Skill Level

Beginner

Finished Size

10 inches W x 15½ inches H

Materials

- 1 sheet 7-count plastic canvas
- Coats & Clark Red Heart Classic worsted weight yarn Art. E267 as listed in color key
- #16 tapestry needle
- 13½-inch x 9½-inch piece colorful felt in coordinating color
- Fabric glue
- Hot-glue gun

Instructions

1. Cut plastic canvas according to graphs (this page and page 150). Cut felt slightly smaller all around than stocking; set aside.

2. Following graphs through step 4, stitch and Overcast cuff, working uncoded background with white Continental Stitches.

3. Stitch and Overcast stocking, working uncoded areas on Santa's beard, hair, pompom and wrist cuff with white Continental Stitches and uncoded areas on teddy bear at bottom of stocking with copper Continental Stitches. *Note: Top portion of stocking will remain unstitched.*

4. When background stitching and Overcasting are completed, use two plies yarn to work French Knots for falling snow, and Straight Stitches and French Knots for teddy bear's facial features.

5. Using fabric glue, attach felt to backside of stocking around edges, leaving top open.

6. Using glue gun, center and glue cuff on top of stocking, overlapping two holes. ✳

COLOR KEY	
Plastic Canvas Yarn	**Yards**
☐ White #1	23
■ Black #12	2
☐ Eggshell #111	1
☐ Yellow #230	2
☐ Sea coral #246	1
☐ Silver #412	2
■ Paddy green #687	7
☐ Pink #737	1
☐ Light periwinkle #827	1
☐ Olympic blue #849	10
■ Cherry red #912	13
■ Cardinal #917	1
Uncoded areas on sign and Santa are white #1 Continental Stitches	
Uncoded areas on teddy bear are copper #289 Continental Stitches	
╱ Cherry red #912 Straight Stitch	
○ White #1 French Knot	
● Black #12 French Knot	
Color numbers given are for Coats & Clark Red Heart Classic worsted weight yarn Art. E267.	

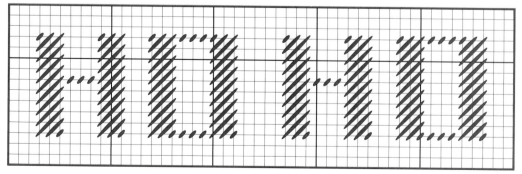

Stocking Cuff
49 holes x 15 holes
Cut 1

Stocking
65 holes x 90 holes
Cut 1

Snowy Golf Buddies

Designs by Joan Green

F or all those men and women who languish during the winter months, stitch this pair of snowmen with golf ball bodies and tee arms!

Skill Level
Beginner

Finished Size
4½ inches W x 4⅛ inches H, excluding hangers

Materials
- ⅛ sheet 7-count plastic canvas
- Coats & Clark Red Heart Classic worsted weight yarn Art. E267 as listed in color key
- Coats & Clark Red Heart Super Saver worsted weight yarn Art. E300 as listed in color key
- #16 tapestry needle
- 4 natural wood-tone golf tees
- Gold glitter stem
- Fabric glue

Instructions
1. Cut plastic canvas according to graphs (page 163).

2. Stitch and Overcast plastic canvas following graphs, working uncoded areas with white Continental Stitches. Work black Cross Stitch noses with 2 plies.

3. When background stitching is completed, use 2 plies black to work Backstitches for mouth and French Knots for eyes. Use 2 plies nickel to Backstitch markings on golf ball bodies.

4. For hangers, cut glitter stem in half. Fold each half and glue ends to top backside of ornaments for hangers. Using photo as a guide, glue tees to backsides for arms. ❋

Graphs on page 163

Signs of Christmas

Designs by Susan Leinberger

Who can resist this trio of winter characters? With their whimsical signs, they are sure to add to your holiday spirit!

Skill Level

Beginner

Finished Size

Polar bear: 5½ inches W x 5½ inches H

Moose: 5½ inches W x 5⅞ inches H

Gingerbread man: 5½ inches W x 5⅜ inches H

Materials

Each character

- ½ sheet 7-count plastic canvas
- Uniek Needloft plastic canvas yarn as listed in color key
- #3 pearl cotton as listed in color key
- #16 tapestry needle
- 6½ inches ⅛-inch-wide red satin ribbon
- Tacky craft glue

Polar bear

- 2 (6mm) round black cabochons
- 2 (½-inch) white pompoms
- 7mm black pompom
- 2 (¼-inch) silver jingle bells
- 2 (1-inch) silver snowflake sequins
- Beading needle
- Transparent thread

Moose

- 2 (6mm) round black cabochons

Gingerbread man

- 2 (6mm) round black cabochons
- 8 inches ¼-inch-wide red satin picot-edged ribbon

Cutting & Stitching

1. Cut plastic canvas according to graphs (pages 153 and 154).

2. Following graphs through step 5, stitch and Overcast holly sprig. Work red French Knots when stitching and Overcasting are completed.

3. Stitch front pieces and signs, working uncoded areas with Continental Stitches as follows: polar bear and signs with white, moose with cinnamon and gingerbread man with maple. Back pieces will remain unstitched.

4. Overcast polar bear and gingerbread man signs with alternating red and white stitches. Overcast moose sign with alternating holly and white stitches.

5. Using black pearl cotton, Backstitch eyebrows on polar bear and mouths on moose and gingerbread man. Work all remaining Backstitches with yarn.

Assembly

1. Use photo as a guide throughout assembly. With beading needle and transparent yarn, attach sequin and jingle bells to polar bear sign where indicated on graph.

2. Cut four 4-inch lengths of red yarn. On backside of each upper corner of polar bear sign, attach one 4-inch length of yarn. Thread lengths from front to back on bear paws where indicated on graph. Adjust lengths, making them even; secure on backside.

3. Tie remaining two lengths in two bows, trimming ends as desired. Glue to bear's paws.

4. Repeat steps 2 and 3 for remaining characters, using white yarn for moose and green yarn for gingerbread man.

5. Thread red picot-edge ribbon from back to front through holes indicated on gingerbread man graph; tie in a bow, trimming ends as desired.

6. For each character, thread one length of ⅛-inch-wide red ribbon through holes at top center of each unstitched back; knotting and gluing on wrong side to secure.

7. Whipstitch front pieces to back pieces following graphs.

8. Glue cabochons to heads for eyes where indicated on graphs. Glue holly sprig to moose. Glue white pompoms to bear's face for muzzle and black pompom just above muzzle for nose. ✽

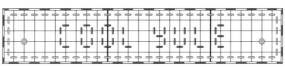

Polar Bear Sign
27 holes x 5 holes
Cut 1

Holly Sprig
5 holes x 3 holes
Cut 1

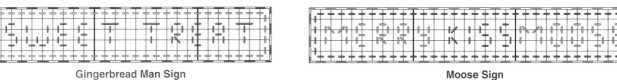

Gingerbread Man Sign
27 holes x 5 holes
Cut 1

Moose Sign
32 holes x 5 holes
Cut 1

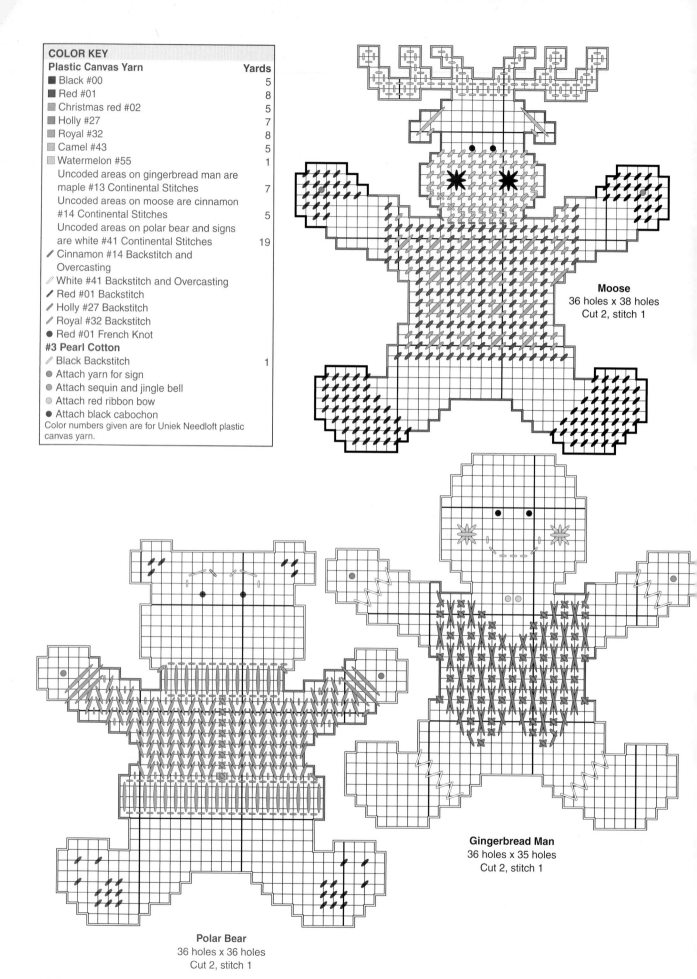

COLOR KEY
Plastic Canvas Yarn   **Yards**
- ■ Black #00 — 5
- ■ Red #01 — 8
- ■ Christmas red #02 — 5
- ■ Holly #27 — 7
- ■ Royal #32 — 8
- ■ Camel #43 — 5
- ■ Watermelon #55 — 1
- Uncoded areas on gingerbread man are maple #13 Continental Stitches — 7
- Uncoded areas on moose are cinnamon #14 Continental Stitches — 5
- Uncoded areas on polar bear and signs are white #41 Continental Stitches — 19
- ✎ Cinnamon #14 Backstitch and Overcasting
- ✎ White #41 Backstitch and Overcasting
- ✎ Red #01 Backstitch
- ✎ Holly #27 Backstitch
- ✎ Royal #32 Backstitch
- ● Red #01 French Knot

#3 Pearl Cotton
- ✎ Black Backstitch — 1
- ● Attach yarn for sign
- ● Attach sequin and jingle bell
- ○ Attach red ribbon bow
- ● Attach black cabochon

Color numbers given are for Uniek Needloft plastic canvas yarn.

Moose
36 holes x 38 holes
Cut 2, stitch 1

Polar Bear
36 holes x 36 holes
Cut 2, stitch 1

Gingerbread Man
36 holes x 35 holes
Cut 2, stitch 1

Gift Mittens

Designs by Alida Macor

Tuck folded-up bills inside the cuffs of these three wintry mittens to give an always appreciated gift!

Skill Level
Beginner

Finished Size
2¾ inches W x 3⅜ inches H

Materials
- Small amount each clear, green, red and white 7-count plastic canvas
- Plastic canvas yarn as listed in color key
- 3 (9-inch) lengths thin gold cord
- #16 tapestry needle

Instructions

1. For mitten fronts, cut one each of mittens A, B and C from clear plastic canvas; for mitten backs, cut one mitten A from red canvas, one mitten B from green canvas and one mitten C from white canvas according to graphs. Mitten backs will remain unstitched.

2. Stitch mitten fronts following graphs, working uncoded areas with Continental Stitches as follows: mitten A with red, mitten B with green and mitten C with white.

3. When background stitching is completed, work French Knot on mitten C with 2 plies yellow.

4. Overcast top edges of mittens A with red, mittens B with green and mittens C with white. Whipstitch fronts to corresponding backs following graphs.

5. For hanger on each mitten, thread one length of gold cord through hole indicated on back piece. Tie ends together in a knot to form a loop for hanging. ✻

Graphs continued on page 163

COLOR KEY	
Plastic Canvas Yarn	**Yards**
☐ White	9
■ Red	8
■ Green	5
Uncoded areas on mitten A are red Continental Stitches	
Uncoded areas on mitten B are green Continental Stitches	
Uncoded areas on mitten C are white Continental Stitches	
○ Yellow French Knot	1
● Attach gold cord hanger	

Mitten A
17 holes x 22 holes
Cut 1 from clear
Stitch as graphed
Cut 1 from red
Do not stitch

Jolly Santa

Design by Lee Lindeman

itting on a shelf or end table, this jolly Santa is perfect for greeting friends and family into your holiday home!

Skill Level

Intermediate

Finished Size

8¼ inches W x 15½ inches H

Sitting: 8¼ inches x 10 inches H

Materials

- 3 sheets 7-count plastic canvas
- Coats & Clark Red Heart Classic worsted weight yarn Art. E267 as listed in color key
- Coats & Clark Red Heart Super Saver worsted weight yarn Art. E300 as listed in color key
- #16 tapestry needle
- 1 package Jumbo Loopy white chenille yarn trim from FloraCraft Corp.
- Wooden craft stick
- Dome-shaped shank buttons:
  2 (⅞-inch) white
  ½-inch white
  ⅜-inch red
- 2¼-inch-wide doll eyeglasses
- Brass or gold-tone buckles:
  ¾-inch x ¾-inch
  2 (¾-inch x ½-inch)
- Sewing needle and white sewing thread
- Small amount felt: black and red
- 2 (⁵⁄₁₆-inch) round brown crystal eyes from Westrim Crafts
- Polyester fiberfill
- Several clean, smooth, small stones or other material for weight
- Tacky craft glue and/or hot-glue gun

Project Note

Refer to photo throughout.

Body, Head & Hat

1. Cut two head and two body pieces from plastic canvas according to graphs (page 158).

2. Following graphs through step 6, stitch body base, front and back. Overcast top edges of body front and back, then Whipstitch wrong sides together along sides edges. Whipstitch bottom edges of body to base.

3. Stuff a small amount of polyester fiberfill in bottom of body; add a handful of small stones or other material for weight. Stuff rest of body with fiberfill.

4. Stitch head front and back following graphs, working uncoded areas with lily pink Continental Stitches. For mustache, cut a few short strands of white yarn; place together and stitch over center of strands with one white stitch where indicated on head front graph with blue line; trim as desired. Glue to secure.

5. Add white Turkey Loop Stitches over completed Continental Stitches to achieve beard and hair of desired fullness. ***Note:*** *Allow room for hat to fit over head.*

6. Overcast bottom edges of head (neck). Whipstitch wrong sides of head pieces together along remaining edges. If desired, work Turkey Loop Stitches over edges to cover.

7. Stuff head with fiberfill through neck opening. Apply glue to one half of craft stick; insert into head through neck. Apply glue to other half of craft stick and insert into stuffing in body through neck opening.

8. Glue red button for nose to Santa's face above mustache. Cut a small half-moon mouth from red felt and glue below mustache. Glue eyes and eyeglasses in place.

9. Stitch hat pieces following graphs, reversing one before stitching. Overcast bottom edges, then Whipstitch wrong sides together along remaining edges. Stuff a little polyester fiberfill in tip of hat. Glue smaller white button to tip of hat. Glue hat on top of Santa's head. Glue chenille trim around brim of hat.

Arms, Legs & Boots

1. Cut arm, leg and boot pieces from plastic canvas according to graphs (page 158).

2. Following graphs through step 3, stitch arms, reversing one of each before stitching. Whipstitch corresponding arms pieces together, stuffing each with a small amount of fiberfill before closing. Glue arms to back of Santa's body at shoulders.

3. Stitch upper legs; Whipstitch together in pairs, stuffing each with a small amount of fiberfill before closing. Repeat with boot tops. Overcast heel ends of each foot piece; Whipstitch feet together in pairs along remaining edges, stuffing each with a small amount of fiberfill.

4. For each leg, glue open end (heel) of foot at right angle to base of boot top. Using red throughout, Whipstitch top edges of boot tops to bottom edges

of upper legs; Whipstitch tops of upper legs to bottom front edge of body.

Finishing

1. Glue chenille trim around each wrist, around bottom of body and around legs where boot tops and upper legs meet.

2. From black felt, cut strip 1½ inches x ⅝ inch; pierce small hole in center of strip to accept tongue of larger buckle. Thread felt strip through larger buckle and glue to center of Santa's black stitched belt. Glue larger white buttons down center of body.

3. From black felt, cut two strips 1⅛ inches x ⅝ inch; pierce small hole in center of each strip to accept tongue of smaller buckle. Thread felt strips through buckles and glue one across top of each foot. ✳

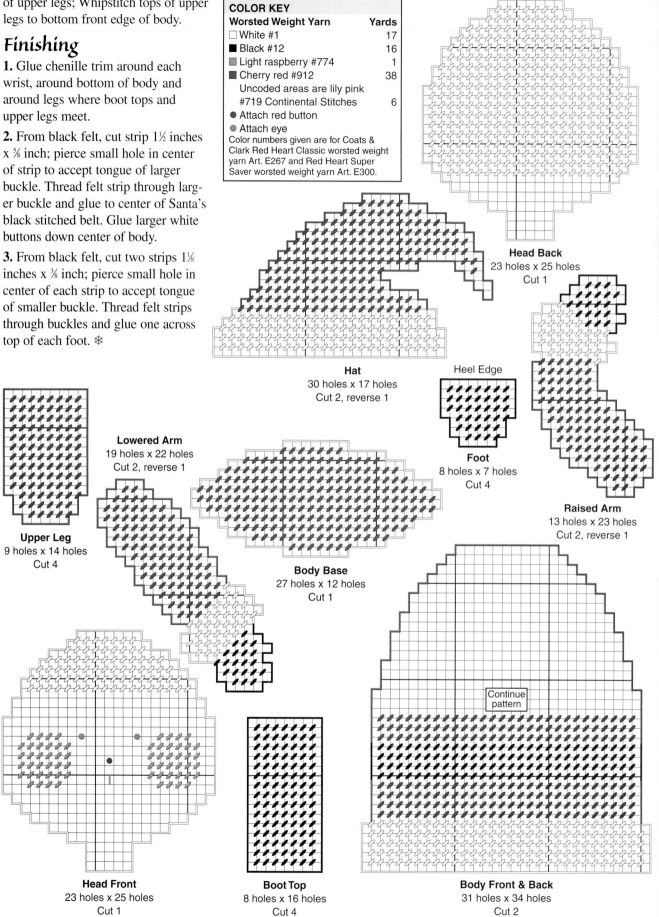

COLOR KEY

Worsted Weight Yarn	Yards
☐ White #1	17
■ Black #12	16
▨ Light raspberry #774	1
▨ Cherry red #912	38
Uncoded areas are lily pink #719 Continental Stitches	6
● Attach red button	
● Attach eye	

Color numbers given are for Coats & Clark Red Heart Classic worsted weight yarn Art. E267 and Red Heart Super Saver worsted weight yarn Art. E300.

Head Back
23 holes x 25 holes
Cut 1

Hat
30 holes x 17 holes
Cut 2, reverse 1

Heel Edge

Foot
8 holes x 7 holes
Cut 4

Raised Arm
13 holes x 23 holes
Cut 2, reverse 1

Lowered Arm
19 holes x 22 holes
Cut 2, reverse 1

Upper Leg
9 holes x 14 holes
Cut 4

Body Base
27 holes x 12 holes
Cut 1

Continue pattern

Head Front
23 holes x 25 holes
Cut 1

Boot Top
8 holes x 16 holes
Cut 4

Body Front & Back
31 holes x 34 holes
Cut 2

158 *Let It Snow! in Plastic Canvas*

Winter Friends

Designs by Lee Lindeman

D ress up your dinner table or a favorite shelf with this set of four cheery projects!

Skill Level

Snowman

Finished Size

6⅛ inches W x 8¾ inches H

Materials

- 1 sheet 7-count plastic canvas
- Coats & Clark Red Heart Classic worsted weight yarn Art. E267 as listed in color key
- 6-strand embroidery floss as listed in color key
- #16 tapestry needle
- 2 (3mm) round black beads
- 3 (6mm) round black cabochons
- Small amount orange craft foam
- Small amount black felt
- 10-inch long strip plaid fabric
- Child's red knit sock
- Sewing needle, and red and black sewing thread
- 1-inch white pompom
- 2 (2½-inch-long) tree twigs
- Small amount fiberfill
- Walnut-size rock
- Hot-glue gun

Instructions

1. Cut plastic canvas according to graphs (pages 162 and 163). For carrot nose, cut two narrow ½-inch-long strips from orange craft foam, cutting one end on each to a point. Cut four mittens from black felt using pattern given.

2. Stitch pieces following graphs, working head back entirely with white Continental Stitches. When background stitching is completed, Backstitch mouth with black embroidery floss.

3. With sewing needle and black sewing thread, attach beads to head front for eyes where indicated on graph.

4. Following graphs through step 5, Whipstitch head front and back together, stuffing with a small amount of fiberfill before closing. On body

front and back, Overcast neck edges and arm edges between dots.

5. Whipstitch base to body front and back, then Whipstitch body sides together up to the waist. Place a small amount of fiberfill in body, tuck in walnut-size rock and add more fiberfill. Continue Whipstitching unworked edges of body sides together, stuffing upper body with fiberfill.

6. Using photo as a guide through step 9, glue neck of head into opening at top of body. Glue nose pieces together, then glue to face. Glue 6mm black cabochons to upper body front for coal buttons.

7. For hat, from top of sock, cut a 2-inch-wide piece long enough to fit snuggly around snowman's head. Using red thread, sew seam along 2-inch edge, then gather top edge. Sew or glue white pompom to top of hat. Turn up cuff; glue hat to snowman's head.

8. Tie plaid fabric around neck for scarf. Glue to secure.

9. Matching edges, glue two mittens together over one end of one twig. Repeat with remaining twig. Glue twigs into arm openings on body.

Santa

Finished Size

6⅜ inches W x 9⅛ inches H

Materials

- 1 sheet 7-count plastic canvas
- Coats & Clark Red Heart Classic worsted weight yarn Art. E267 as listed in color key
- #16 tapestry needle
- 2 (3mm) round black beads
- 5mm red bead
- 2 (½-inch) white dome buttons
- Sewing needle and black thread
- Small amount each red and black felt
- Small amount white faux fur or hair
- White Rainbow Plush felt from Kunin
- 1-inch white pompom

- 2 (2½-inch-long) tree twigs
- Small amount fiberfill
- Walnut-size rock
- Hot-glue gun

Instructions

1. Cut plastic canvas according to graphs (pages 161 and 162). Cut four mittens from black felt, one hat from red felt, one mustache from white plush felt, one beard and one hair piece from white faux fur or hair using patterns given.

2. Stitch pieces following graphs. With sewing needle and black sewing thread, attach 3mm black beads to head front for eyes where indicated on graph.

3. Use photo as a guide through step 7. Following graphs and steps 4–6 for snowman, assemble Santa.

4. Glue red bead to head front for nose where indicated on graph. Glue white dome buttons to upper body front. Glue mustache and beard to face. Glue hair to center back of head, wrapping ends around edges.

5. Glue a ½-inch-wide strip of white plush felt completely around Santa where indicated on body graph, cutting away excess as necessary.

6. Overlap and glue straight edges of hat together, forming a cone to fit Santa's head. Glue a ⅜-inch-wide strip of white plush felt around bottom edge of hat. Glue pompom to top of hat. Place hat on head.

7. Matching edges, glue two mittens together over one end of one twig. Repeat with remaining twig. Glue a ¼-inch-wide strip of white plush felt around wrist of each mitten. Glue twigs into arm openings on body.

Elf

Finished Size

5½ inches W x 7¾ inches H

Materials

- 1 sheet 7-count plastic canvas
- 6-strand embroidery floss as listed in color key

- Coats & Clark Red Heart Classic worsted weight yarn Art. E267 as listed in color key
- #16 tapestry needle
- 14 inches ¹⁄₁₆-inch-wide gold metallic yarn
- 4 inches ⅜-inch-wide gold ribbon
- 2 (3mm) round black beads
- 3 (⅜-inch) gold jingle bells
- Sewing needle and black sewing thread
- Small amount jute minicurl doll hair
- Small amount green craft foam
- Candy cane button
- Pinking shears
- Small amount fiberfill
- Walnut-size rock
- Hot-glue gun

Instructions

1. Cut plastic canvas according to graphs (this page and page 162). Cut four mittens and hat brim from green craft foam using patterns given, using pinking shears to cut outside edge of brim.

2. Stitch pieces following graphs. When background stitching is completed, Backstitch mouth with black embroidery floss; work lily pink French Knot for nose.

3. With sewing needle and black sewing thread, attach beads to head front for eyes where indicated on graph.

4. Use photo as a guide through step 9. Following graphs and steps 4–6 for snowman, assemble elf.

5. Cut jute minicurl hair into short pieces, then glue to head front, back and sides where emerald green and lily pink stitching meet.

6. Slip hat brim over head and glue in place on top of curls. For hatband, wrap a 5-inch-length of ¹⁄₁₆-inch-wide gold metallic yarn around head just above hat brim; trim to fit and glue in place.

7. Glue ⅜-inch gold ribbon around waist of body. Glue one jingle bell to center top edge of elf hat. Glue remaining two jingle bells to upper body front for buttons.

8. Tie remaining length of ¹⁄₁₆-inch-wide gold metallic yarn in a bow around neck. Trim ends.

9. Matching edges, glue two mittens together over one end of one twig. Repeat with remaining twig. Glue twigs into arm openings on body. Glue candy cane button to one mitten.

Reindeer

Finished Size
4¾ inches W x 10¼ inches H

Materials
- 1 sheet 7-count plastic canvas
- Coats & Clark Red Heart Classic worsted weight yarn Art. E267 as listed in color key
- 6-strand embroidery floss as listed in color key
- #16 tapestry needle
- 2 (6mm) brown crystal eyes from Westrim Crafts
- Small amount dark heather brown Rainbow Plush felt from Kunin
- 12mm black animal D-nose from Darice
- 2 (3½-inch-long) tree twigs
- 2 (2½-inch-long) tree twigs
- 1-inch off-white or brown pompom
- 8 inches ⅜-inch-wide red satin ribbon
- Small amount fiberfill
- Walnut-size rock
- Hot-glue gun

Instructions

1. Cut plastic canvas according to graphs (pages 162 and 163). Cut four ½-inch circles from dark heather brown plush felt for reindeer hooves.

2. Stitch pieces following graphs, working head back, body back and both ear backs entirely with mid brown Continental Stitches. When background stitching is completed, embroider mouth with black floss.

3. Using mid brown through step 5, Overcast top edge of both head front and head back. Whipstitch wrong

sides of head together along remaining edges; stuff with a small amount of fiberfill.

4. On body front and back, Overcast neck edges and arm edges between dots. For each ear, Whipstitch wrong sides of one ear front to one ear back.

5. Whipstitch base to body front and back, then Whipstitch body sides together up to the waist. Place a small amount of fiberfill in body, tuck in walnut-size rock and add more fiberfill. Continue Whipstitching unworked body sides together; stuff upper body with fiberfill.

6. Using photo as a guide through step 9, glue neck of head into opening at top of body.

7. Glue eyes and nose to head where indicated on graph. Tie red satin ribbon in a bow around neck; trim ends.

8. Glue both 3⅓-inch-long twigs into head top for antlers. Glue ears to head.

9. Glue two hooves together over one end of one 2½-inch twig. Repeat with remaining twig. Glue twigs into arm openings on body. ❊

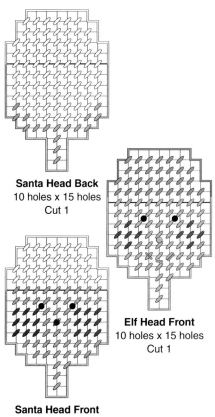

Santa Head Back
10 holes x 15 holes
Cut 1

Elf Head Front
10 holes x 15 holes
Cut 1

Santa Head Front
10 holes x 15 holes
Cut 1

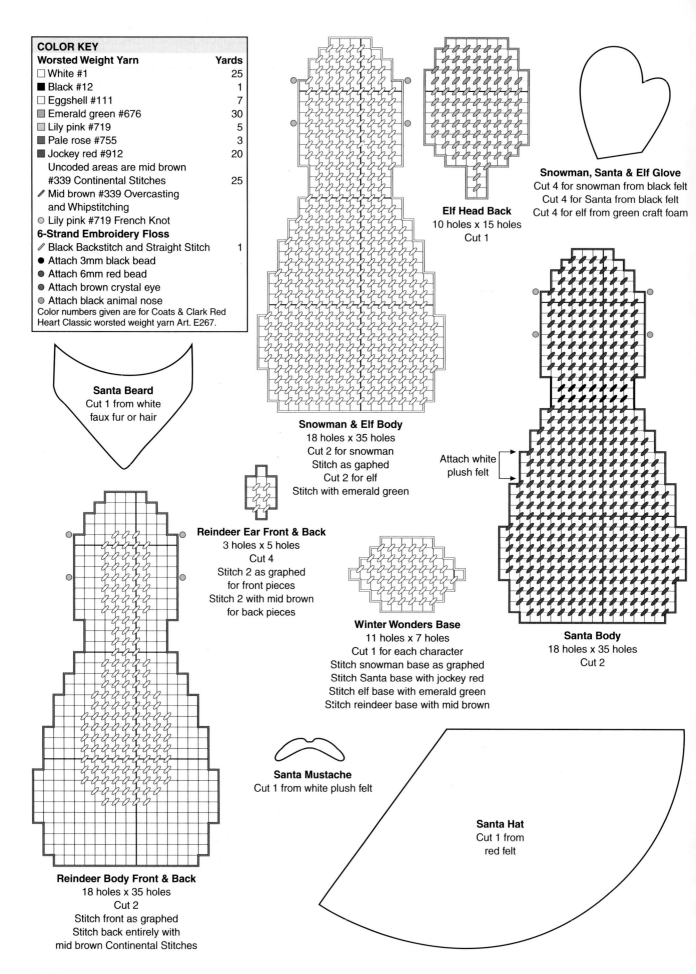

COLOR KEY

Worsted Weight Yarn	Yards
□ White #1	25
■ Black #12	1
□ Eggshell #111	7
▨ Emerald green #676	30
▨ Lily pink #719	5
▨ Pale rose #755	3
▨ Jockey red #912	20
Uncoded areas are mid brown #339 Continental Stitches	25

✐ Mid brown #339 Overcasting
   and Whipstitching
○ Lily pink #719 French Knot

6-Strand Embroidery Floss

✐ Black Backstitch and Straight Stitch	1

● Attach 3mm black bead
● Attach 6mm red bead
● Attach brown crystal eye
● Attach black animal nose

Color numbers given are for Coats & Clark Red Heart Classic worsted weight yarn Art. E267.

Santa Beard
Cut 1 from white
faux fur or hair

Snowman & Elf Body
18 holes x 35 holes
Cut 2 for snowman
Stitch as gaphed
Cut 2 for elf
Stitch with emerald green

Elf Head Back
10 holes x 15 holes
Cut 1

Snowman, Santa & Elf Glove
Cut 4 for snowman from black felt
Cut 4 for Santa from black felt
Cut 4 for elf from green craft foam

Reindeer Ear Front & Back
3 holes x 5 holes
Cut 4
Stitch 2 as graphed
for front pieces
Stitch 2 with mid brown
for back pieces

Winter Wonders Base
11 holes x 7 holes
Cut 1 for each character
Stitch snowman base as graphed
Stitch Santa base with jockey red
Stitch elf base with emerald green
Stitch reindeer base with mid brown

Attach white
plush felt

Santa Body
18 holes x 35 holes
Cut 2

Reindeer Body Front & Back
18 holes x 35 holes
Cut 2
Stitch front as graphed
Stitch back entirely with
mid brown Continental Stitches

Santa Mustache
Cut 1 from white plush felt

Santa Hat
Cut 1 from
red felt

162   *Let It Snow! in Plastic Canvas*

Reindeer Head Front & Back
10 holes x 15 holes
Cut 2
Stitch front as graphed
Stitch back entirely with
mid brown Continental Stitches

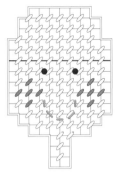

Snowman Head Front & Back
10 holes x 15 holes
Cut 2
Stitch front as graphed
Stitch back entirely with
white Continental Stitches

Santa Hair
Cut 1 from
faux fur or hair

Elf Hat Brim
Cut 1 from
green craft foam

Cut out
center circle

Gift Mittens

Continued from page 155

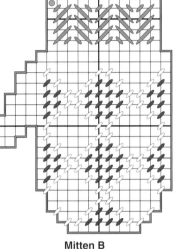

Mitten B
17 holes x 22 holes
Cut 1 from clear
Stitch as graphed
Cut 1 from green
Do not stitch

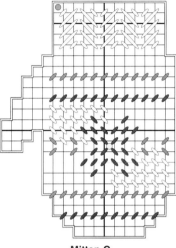

Mitten C
17 holes x 22 holes
Cut 1 from clear
Stitch as graphed
Cut 1 from white
Do not stitch

Snowy Golf Buddies

Continued from page 151

COLOR KEY	
Worsted Weight Yarn	**Yards**
■ Black #312	2
▨ Silver #412	3
▨ Paddy green #686	1
▨ Grass green #687	1
▨ Pink #737	1
■ Cherry red #912	2
Uncoded areas are white #1	
Continental Stitches	7
⁄ White #1 Overcasting	
╱ Black #312 Backstitch	
⁄ Nickel #401 Backstitch	1
● Black #312 French Knot	

Color numbers given are for Coats & Clark
Red Heart Classic worsted weight yarn
Art. E267 and Super Saver worsted weight
yarn Art. E300.

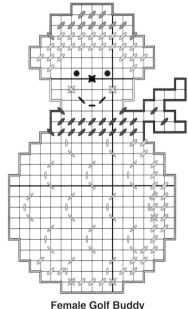

Female Golf Buddy
17 holes x 27 holes
Cut 1

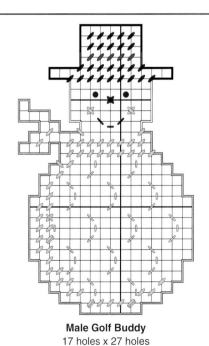

Male Golf Buddy
17 holes x 27 holes
Cut 1

Chubby Angel & Santa

Designs by Lee Lindeman

With their plump, round bodies and rosy cheeks, this pair of large ornaments is sure to warm your heart!

Skill Level

Intermediate

Finished Size

Angel: 5 inches W x 9½ inches H

Santa: 3¾ inches W x 9¼ inches H

Materials

Each Ornament

- 1 sheet 7-count plastic canvas
- Coats & Clark Red Heart Classic worsted weight yarn Art. E267 as listed in color key
- Coats & Clark Red Heart Super Saver worsted weight yarn Art. E300 as listed in color key
- #16 tapestry needle
- 2 (3mm) round black beads
- Small amount fiberfill
- 18 inches gold metallic cord or yarn
- Sewing needle and black sewing thread
- Hot-glue gun

Angel

- Metallic yarn as listed in color key
- 3 (⅝-inch) crystal stars
- 1 yard white lace
- 4¾ inch x 2¼-inch piece white stiff fabric or craft foam
- Dental floss
- Fabric glue

Santa

- ⅞-inch red dome button
- 3 (⅞-inch) white dome buttons
- ¾-inch x ½-inch gold buckle

Cutting & Stitching

1. Cut plastic canvas according to graphs (page 166). Cut wings from white stiff fabric or craft foam using pattern given.

2. Stitch pieces following graphs, working lower portion of Santa head back entirely with lily pink Continental Stitches, eliminating light raspberry stitching. Work uncoded areas on Santa pieces with jockey red Continental Stitches.

3. With sewing needle and black sewing thread, attach beads to head front for eyes where indicated on graph. Center buckle on Santa's belt front and sew on with black yarn.

4. Using photo as a guide, for angel hair, using maize work ½-inch Loop Stitches over maize Continental Stitches on head front and back. For Santa, using white, work ½-inch Loop Stitches for mustache and bangs and 1-inch Loop Stitches for beard, and remainder of hair.

Assembly

1. Use photo as a guide throughout assembly. Working with corresponding pieces throughout assembly, Whipstitch head front and back pieces together, stuffing with a small amount of fiberfill before closing. Work Loop Stitches for hair over edges.

2. Using adjacent colors throughout, Overcast top and bottom edges of bodies, then Whipstitch front and back pieces together along side edges. Matching edges, Whipstitch arm and leg pieces together.

3. Glue necks on heads into openings at tops of bodies. Stuff bodies with fiberfill.

4. Glue legs into bottom openings of bodies, gluing bodies shut between legs.

5. Cut two 12-inch lengths and two 6-inch lengths of lace. Using fabric glue through step 6, glue one 12-inch length around bottom edge of angel body; glue and overlap ends, cutting away excess.

6. Using sewing needle and dental floss, gather each remaining length of lace. Tie 12-inch length around neck and 6-inch lengths around wrists, overlapping and gluing ends together. Glue wings to back below collar.

7. For hangers, thread 18-inch length of gold yarn or cord through top hole of each ornament. Tie ends together in a knot to form loops for hanging.

8. Using hot glue through step 9, glue arms to bodies. Glue red button for nose above mustache on Santa. Glue one white button to front of hat at tip and remaining two to body above belt.

9. Glue one star to front of angel's hat at tip; glue remaining two stars to body front. ❋

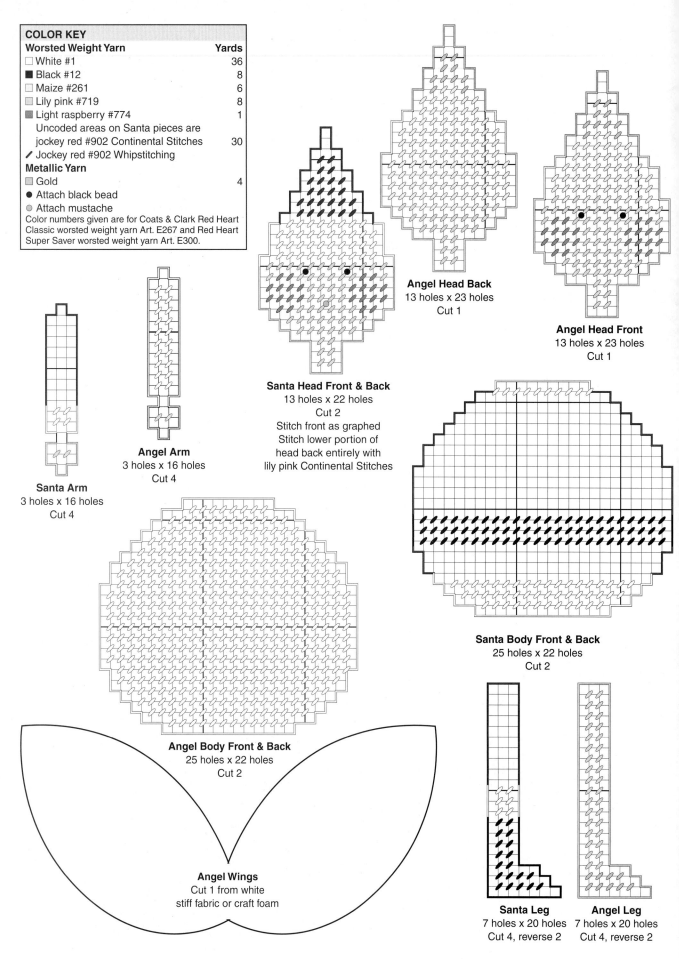

COLOR KEY

Worsted Weight Yarn	Yards
☐ White #1	36
■ Black #12	8
☐ Maize #261	6
☐ Lily pink #719	8
▨ Light raspberry #774	1
Uncoded areas on Santa pieces are jockey red #902 Continental Stitches	30
╱ Jockey red #902 Whipstitching	
Metallic Yarn	
☐ Gold	4
● Attach black bead	
◯ Attach mustache	

Color numbers given are for Coats & Clark Red Heart Classic worsted weight yarn Art. E267 and Red Heart Super Saver worsted weight yarn Art. E300.

Angel Head Back
13 holes x 23 holes
Cut 1

Angel Head Front
13 holes x 23 holes
Cut 1

Santa Head Front & Back
13 holes x 22 holes
Cut 2
Stitch front as graphed
Stitch lower portion of
head back entirely with
lily pink Continental Stitches

Santa Arm
3 holes x 16 holes
Cut 4

Angel Arm
3 holes x 16 holes
Cut 4

Santa Body Front & Back
25 holes x 22 holes
Cut 2

Angel Body Front & Back
25 holes x 22 holes
Cut 2

Angel Wings
Cut 1 from white
stiff fabric or craft foam

Santa Leg
7 holes x 20 holes
Cut 4, reverse 2

Angel Leg
7 holes x 20 holes
Cut 4, reverse 2

Kitty & Pup Treat Holders

Designs by Kristine Loffredo

Delight the youngest members of your family with this pair of animal treat holders! They're just the right size for filling with Christmas candies!

Skill Level

Beginner

Finished Size

Kitty: 4¾ inches W x 7¾ inches H

Pup Holder: 6 inches W x 8¼ inches H

Materials

- 2 sheets Uniek QuickCount 7-count plastic canvas
- Uniek Needloft plastic canvas yarn as listed in color key
- Kreinik Medium #16 Braid as listed in color key
- #16 tapestry needle
- 6 (8mm) red faceted beads
- 2 (15mm) oval black movable eyes
- 2 (18mm) round black movable eyes
- Sewing needle and green sewing thread
- Hot-glue gun

Cutting & Stitching

1. Cut plastic canvas according to graphs. Cut two 28-hole x 16-hole pieces for holder bottoms. Holder bottoms will remain unstitched.

2. Stitch holder front and sides as graphed for kitty; stitch pup holder front and sides replacing royal with bright purple.

3. Work hats with Reverse Continental Stitches, then Overcast all edges following graphs. Work ⅜-inch Turkey Loop Stitches for cuffs and pompoms. Cut loops and fray yarn, trimming as desired.

4. Stitch remaining pieces following graphs, working uncoded areas on kitty with lemon Continental Stitches.

5. Following graphs, Overcast kitty and pup bodies around sides and top from dot to dot. Overcast top edges of holder front and side pieces with adjacent colors. Overcast leaves, paws and muzzles following graphs.

6. When background stitching and

Overcasting are completed, work Backstitches and Straight Stitches on bodies, muzzles and paws.

Assembly

1. Use photo as guide throughout assembly. Following graphs, Whip-stitch corresponding box fronts to box sides, then Whipstitch to box backs (lower portion of bodies). Whipstitch front, backs and sides to unstitched box bottoms.

2. Sew leaves to box fronts with sewing needle and green sewing thread. Center and glue three red beads in a cluster to each box front between leaves.

3. For each holder, glue hat to head between ears, tilting slightly. Glue paws to body sides and to top edge of box, so they are hanging out over sides.

4. Center and glue kitty muzzle to head above mouth. Center and glue pup muzzle so bottom edge is just below neck area.

5. Glue oval eyes to kitty head and round eyes to pup head. ❋

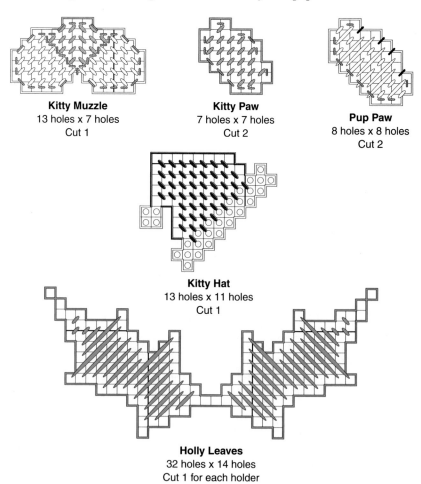

Kitty Muzzle
13 holes x 7 holes
Cut 1

Kitty Paw
7 holes x 7 holes
Cut 2

Pup Paw
8 holes x 8 holes
Cut 2

Kitty Hat
13 holes x 11 holes
Cut 1

Holly Leaves
32 holes x 14 holes
Cut 1 for each holder

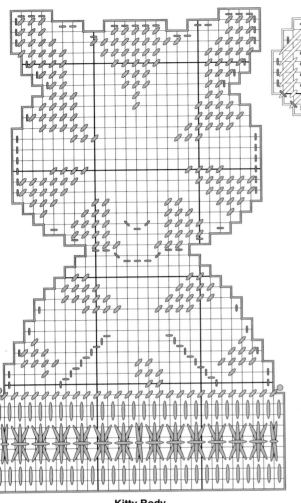

Kitty Body
28 holes x 45 holes
Cut 1

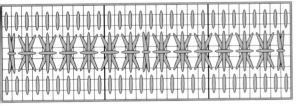

Kitty Holder Front
28 holes x 9 holes
Cut 1

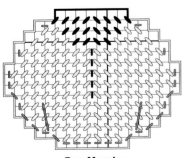

Pup Muzzle
17 holes x 13 holes
Cut 1

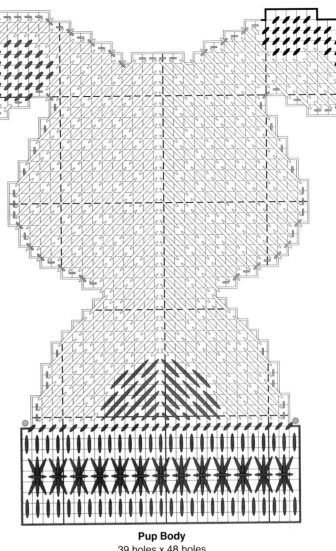

Pup Body
39 holes x 48 holes
Cut 1

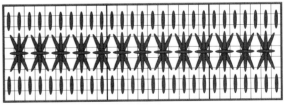

Pup Holder Front
27 holes x 9 holes
Cut 1

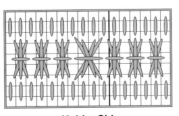

Holder Side
16 holes x 9 holes
Cut 2 for each holder
Stitch 2 as graphed for kitty holder
Stitch 2 with bright purple
for pup holder

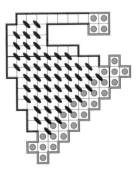

Pup Hat
12 holes x 14 holes
Cut 1

Candy Cane Friends

Designs by Janelle Giese

Children love a Christmas tree decorated with red-and-white candy canes! Stitch a dozen of each friendly holder to add to their delight!

Skill Level

Beginner

Finished Size

Santa: 4½ inches W x 3½ inches H

Snow lady: 4 inches W x 4¼ inches H

Reindeer: 4⅛ inches W x 4⅛ inches H

Materials

- ⅔ sheet Uniek QuickCount 7-count plastic canvas
- Uniek Needloft plastic canvas yarn as listed in color key
- #5 pearl cotton as listed in color key
- DMC 6-strand embroidery floss as listed in color key
- #16 tapestry needle
- 3 (⅜-inch) gold jingle bells
- 3 (9-inch) lengths ⅛-inch white elastic cord

Instructions

1. Cut plastic canvas according to graphs.

2. Stitch and Overcast pieces following graphs, working uncoded areas with white Continental Stitches.

3. When background stitching is completed, work Cross Stitches on cheeks with 2 plies light salmon floss. Work black pearl cotton embroidery.

4. Using full strand white yarn,

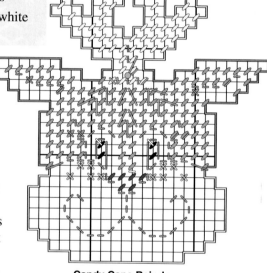

Candy Cane Reindeer
27 holes x 27 holes
Cut 1

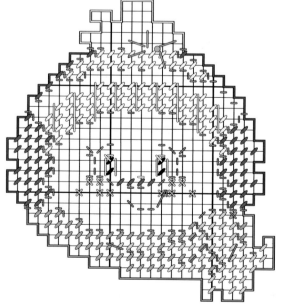

Candy Cane Snow Lady
26 holes x 28 holes
Cut 1

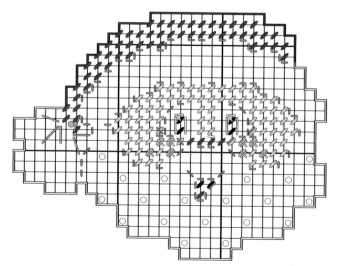

Candy Cane Santa
30 holes x 23 holes
Cut 1

work Straight Stitches for ribbing lines on snow lady's hat and French Knots on Santa's beard. Use 1 ply holly to Straight Stitch greenery.

5. Using 1 ply throughout, for eye color around pupils, work sail blue Straight Stitches on Santa and snow lady, and cinnamon Straight Stitches on reindeer. Use white to Straight Stitch highlight at each nose and to work Pin Stitches for eye highlights, splitting a black stitch as indicated.

6. Using pearl cotton, attach one jingle bell to each motif where indicated on graphs.

7. For candy cane holders, make a double ½-inch loop of elastic by drawing cord through back of stitching between eyes, allowing loop to extend ½ inch. Thread ends of elastic into back of stitching to secure.

8. Place a group of candy canes or one large peppermint stick into elastic loop. ❋

COLOR KEY	
Plastic Canvas Yarn	**Yards**
■ Black #00	1
■ Red #01	4
▨ Maple #13	4
▨ Moss #25	1
■ Holly #27	3
☐ Beige #40	4
▨ Flesh tone #56	2
Uncoded areas are white #41	
Continental Stitches	16
⁄ White #41 Straight Stitch, Pin Stitch and Overcasting	
⁄ Cinnamon #14 Straight Stitch	1
⁄ Holly #27 Straight Stitch	
⁄ Sail blue #35 Straight Stitch	1
○ White #41 French Knot	
#5 Pearl Cotton	
⁄ Black Backstitch and Straight Stitch	7
6-Strand Embroidery Floss	
✕ Light salmon #761 Cross Stitch	1
● Attach jingle bell	
Color numbers given are for Uniek Needloft plastic canvas yarn and DMC 6-strand embroidery floss.	

Santa Canister

Design by Janelle Giese

Y ou'll find many uses for this festive canister! In the kitchen, it's perfect for holding holiday goodies! You can also use it as a gift package, tissue holder or fireplace match holder!

Skill Level

Beginner

Materials

- 1 sheet Uniek QuickCount stiff 7-count plastic canvas
- 1 artist-size sheet Uniek QuickCount regular 7-count plastic canvas
- 2 (6-inch) Uniek QuickShape plastic canvas radial circles
- Uniek Needloft plastic canvas yarn as listed in color key
- Honeysuckle rayon chenille yarn by Elmore-Pisgah Inc. as listed in color key
- Kreinik Heavy (#32) Braid as listed in color key
- #5 pearl cotton as listed in color key
- DMC 6-strand embroidery floss as listed in color key
- #16 tapestry needle
- 3 (⅜-inch) gold jingle bells
- Thick white glue (optional)

Finished Size

Santa motif: 12 inches W x 7⅝ inches H

Candle: 11⅛ inches H x 5¾ inches in diameter

Project Note

Use a double-strand for all stitching with rayon chenille yarn.

Candle

1. Cut lid side, candle side and flame from regular plastic canvas according to graphs (this page and page 174).

2. For lid top, cut cross bars from very center of one 6-inch plastic canvas radial circle, leaving a small hole. For candle base, cut one row of holes from outside edge of remaining radial circle. Candle base will remain unstitched.

3. Following graphs through step 8, stitch candle side, overlapping five holes before stitching and working uncoded areas with red Continental Stitches.

4. Using Christmas red throughout, Overcast top edge. Whipstitch bottom edge to unstitched base.

5. Stitch and Overcast candle flame, then work gold braid Straight Stitches.

6. Stitch lid top with Continental Stitches as follows: Using burgundy Overcast inside edge, then work next four rows. Overcast outside edge with Christmas red, then work first row, nearest edge. Skip next (second) row, then using red, stitch remaining rows to burgundy stitching.

7. Work lid side, overlapping five holes before stitching. Using Christmas red, Overcast bottom edge, then Whipstitch top edge to unworked row on lid top.

8. Insert wick of flame into center hole of lid. Turn lid over; Whipstitch bottom hole on wick in place with burgundy.

Santa

1. Cut Santa from stiff plastic canvas according to graph (page 174).

2. Stitch and Overcast piece following graph, working uncoded background on face with flesh tone Continental Stitches and uncoded areas on hat and

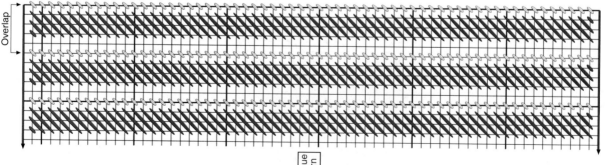

Candle Side
120 holes x 62 holes
Cut 1 from regular

Overlap

Continue pattern

To: Santa
From: Grant

COLOR KEY	
Plastic Canvas Yarn	**Yards**
■ Black #00	6
■ Christmas red #02	78
Burdundy #03	3
■ Tangerine #11	1
□ Lemon #20	1
■ Christmas green #28	5
■ Forest #29	2
□ White #41	28
Uncoded areas on candle side are red #01 Continental Stitches	44
Uncoded background on Santa face is flesh tone #56 Continental Stitches	4
⁄ White #41 Straight Stitch	
Rayon Chenille Yarn	
□ White #1	32
■ Ruby #23	15
Uncoded areas on Santa hat and body are red #22 Continental Stitches	14
Heavy (#32) Braid	
■ Gold #002	6
⁄ Gold #002 Straight Stitch	
#5 Pearl Cotton	
⁄ Black Backstitch and Straight Stitch	7
6-Strand Embroidery Floss	
✕ Medium salmon #3712 Cross Stitch	1
● Attach jingle bell	

Color numbers given are for Uniek Needloft plastic canvas yarn, Elmore-Pisgah Honeysuckle rayon chenille yarn, Kreinik Medium (#32) Braid and DMC 6-strand embroidery floss.

suit with red chenille yarn Continental Stitches.

3. Work two stitches (two double strands) per hole for beard and mustache as indicated. Work Christmas green Straight Stitches for holly leaves.

4. When background stitching and Overcasting are completed, work Cross Stitches on cheeks with 2 plies medium salmon floss. Work black pearl cotton embroidery, then work bow highlights with one ply white plastic canvas yarn.

5. Attach jingle bells with black pearl cotton where indicated on graph.

6. Using photo as a guide, place Santa on candle front, making sure bottom edges are even; tack in place at a few center black Backstitches with black pearl cotton. If desired, for extra security, glue in place with a vertical line of glue. ❄

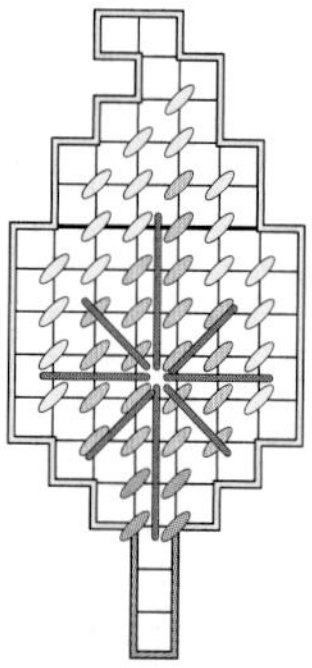

Candle Flame
7 holes x 15 holes
Cut 1 from regular

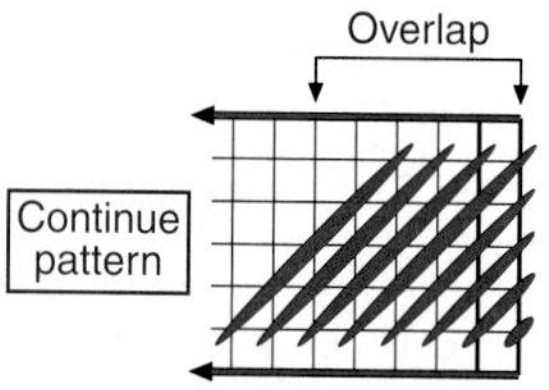

Overlap
Continue pattern

Lid Side
111 holes x 6 holes
Cut 1 from regular

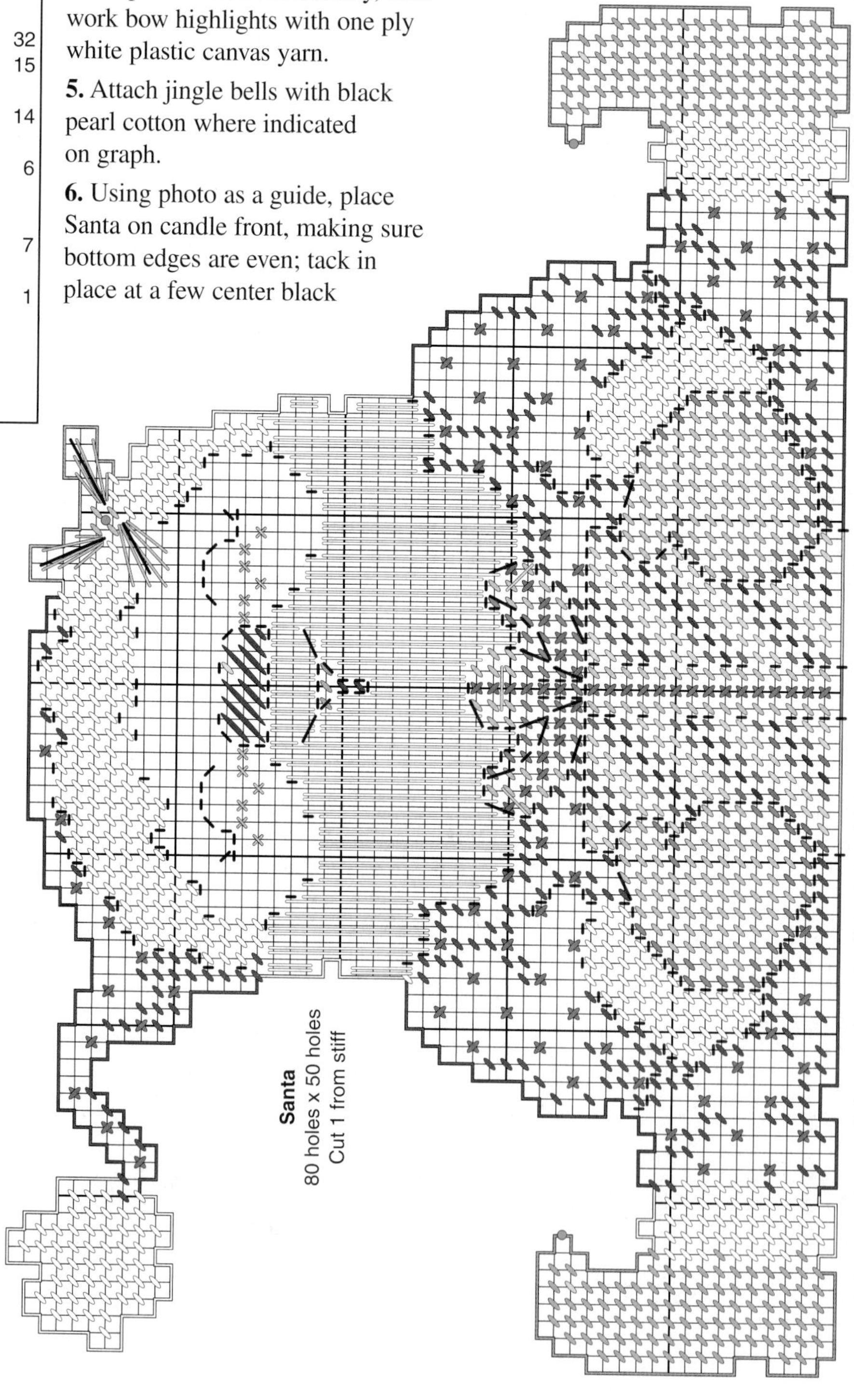

Santa
80 holes x 50 holes
Cut 1 from stiff

Christmas Paper Roll Holders

Designs by Christina Laws

Dress up your kitchen and bathroom with this pair of creative paper holders—one for a spare toilet tissue roll and the other for paper towels.

Skill Level
Beginner

Finished Size
Paper Towel Holder: 16½ inches H x 7¼ inches in diameter

Toilet Paper Holder: 9 inches H x 4¾ inches in diameter

Materials
- 3 sheets 7-count plastic canvas
- Worsted weight yarn as listed in color key
- #16 tapestry needle
- Fiberfill

Paper Towel Holder

1. Cut plastic canvas according to graphs, cutting out hole on base top only.

2. Stitch Santa pieces following graph, reversing one Santa before stitching and leaving tabs unstitched. Work two stitches per hole for beard, hair, hand and wrist cuff where indicated.

3. When background stitching is completed, work red Straight Stitches for mouths and black French Knots for eyes. Using white, work Backstitches above belts, Straight Stitches for mustaches and Cross Stitches for buttons.

4. Whipstitch wrong sides of Santa pieces together following graph.

5. Stitch base, stand and cap pieces following graphs, working base top with white Diagonal Mosaic Stitches as graphed and base bottom completely with green Diagonal Mosaic Stitches.

6. Whipstitch base sides together following graphs, then using green through step 9, Whipstitch sides to base bottom.

7. For stand, Whipstitch sides together, then Whipstitch sides to top; Overcast bottom edges. Whipstitch assembled stand to hole on base top where indicated on stand graph with blue line.

8. Align edges of base top with top edges of base sides, then glue bottom of stand to wrong side of base bottom; Whipstitch top to sides, stuffing with fiberfill before closing.

9. For cap, Overcast inside edges of bottom. Whipstitch sides together, then Whipstitch sides to bottom. Insert tab on Santa into opening on top, then Whipstitch Santa to opening where indicated on Santa graph with pink line. Whipstitch top to sides.

Toilet Paper Holder

1. Cut pieces following graphs, cutting out hole on base top only.

2. Stitch Christmas trees following graph, leaving tabs unstitched. When background stitching is completed, work red Straight Stitches.

3. Whipstitch wrong sides of Christmas trees together following graph.

4. Following steps 5–9 of paper towel holder, stitch and assemble toilet paper holder, replacing green with red and Whipstitching tree in place to cap top. ✳

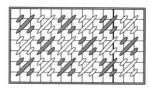

COLOR KEY

Worsted Weight Yarn	Yards
■ Green	60
□ White	52
■ Red	33
■ Black	2
▨ Peach	1
□ Gold	1
▥ Brown	1
⟋ White Backstitch, Straight Stitch, and Cross Stitch	
⟋ Red Straight Stitch	
● Black French Knot	

Cap Side
13 holes x 7 holes
Cut 4 for paper towel holder
Stitch as graphed
Cut 4 for toilet paper holder,
replacing green with red

Stand Top
5 holes x 5 holes
Cut 1 for paper towel holder
Stitch as graphed
Cut 1 for toilet paper holder
Stitch with red

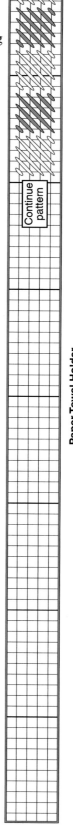

**Paper Towel Holder
Base Side B**
80 holes x 5 holes
Cut 1

Continue pattern

**Paper Towel Holder
Base Side A**
81 holes x 5 holes
Cut 1

Continue pattern

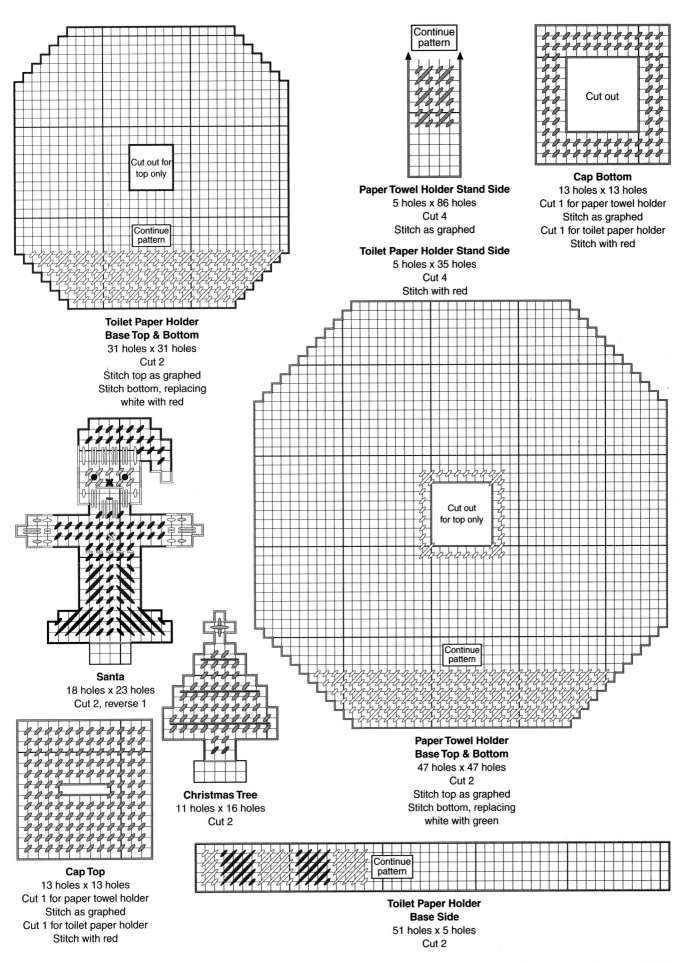

Continue pattern

Paper Towel Holder Stand Side
5 holes x 86 holes
Cut 4
Stitch as graphed

Toilet Paper Holder Stand Side
5 holes x 35 holes
Cut 4
Stitch with red

Cap Bottom
13 holes x 13 holes
Cut 1 for paper towel holder
Stitch as graphed
Cut 1 for toilet paper holder
Stitch with red

Cut out

Cut out for top only

Continue pattern

Toilet Paper Holder Base Top & Bottom
31 holes x 31 holes
Cut 2
Stitch top as graphed
Stitch bottom, replacing white with red

Paper Towel Holder Base Top & Bottom
47 holes x 47 holes
Cut 2
Stitch top as graphed
Stitch bottom, replacing white with green

Santa
18 holes x 23 holes
Cut 2, reverse 1

Christmas Tree
11 holes x 16 holes
Cut 2

Continue pattern

Toilet Paper Holder Base Side
51 holes x 5 holes
Cut 2

Cap Top
13 holes x 13 holes
Cut 1 for paper towel holder
Stitch as graphed
Cut 1 for toilet paper holder
Stitch with red

Folk-Art Greeting Girl

Design by Susan Leinberger

ivid Christmas colors and a variety of stitches make this holiday project bold and alive! Create it to decorate a door or wall in your home!

Skill Level

Beginner

Finished Size

13⅜ inches W x 17½ inches H

Materials

- 2 sheets 7-count plastic canvas
- Coats & Clark Red Heart Classic worsted weight yarn Art. E267 as listed in color key
- #16 tapestry needle
- 4 (½-inch) gold jingle bells
- Hot-glue gun or tacky craft glue

Instructions

1. Cut plastic canvas according to graphs (this page and pages 180 and 181).

2. Stitch and Overcast holly leaves following graph, working Straight Stitches last.

3. Stitch greeting girl and sign front pieces following graph, working uncoded areas on dog with cornmeal Continental Stitches and uncoded areas on border of sign with soft navy Continental Stitches. Back pieces will remain unstitched.

4. When background stitching is completed, work Backstitches, Straight Stitches and French Knots. Work Turkey Loop Stitches (Fig. 1) for bangs and collar.

5. Work each Lark's Head Knot on girl's head with a 12-inch length of medium brown. Divide tails of Lark's Head Knots into three groups of two; braid until approximately 2½ inches long. Tie a bow at end of braid with a 6-inch length cherry red, trimming ends of bow and braid as desired.

Assembly

1. Use photo as a guide throughout assembly. Cut four 4-inch lengths of cherry red. Thread one jingle bell to center of each strand. Thread both ends of one length from front to back through one hole indicated with blue dot on sign graph, leaving a ¾-inch to 1-inch loop. Secure with a knot on backside.

2. Repeat for last three lengths, threading through remaining holes.

3. Whipstitch front pieces to back pieces following graphs.

4. For hat tassel, cut eight 4-inch lengths of cherry red. Thread all eight strands halfway through hole at tip of hat. Fold ends down and wrap a 6-inch length of yellow several times around tassel under bottom edge of hat tip, knotting on back of tassel.

5. Cut two 8-inch lengths cherry red; tie each in a bow, trimming ends as desired. Glue one bow on each side of sign just above blue dots. Glue two holly leaves above each bow.

6. Cut two 9-inch lengths of cherry red, then work Lark's Head Knots on sign where indicated with arrows. Thread ends of each from back to front through corresponding holes on sled runners, indicated with arrows. Adjust lengths so they hang evenly; tie each in a bow. Trim ends as needed.

7. Hang assembled project as desired. ✳

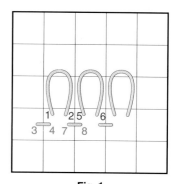

Fig. 1
Turkey Loop Stitch
Bring needle up at 1. Leaving a loop above canvas, bring needle down at 2. Anchor loop by coming up at 3 and going down at 4.

Holly Leaf
5 holes x 5 holes
Cut 4

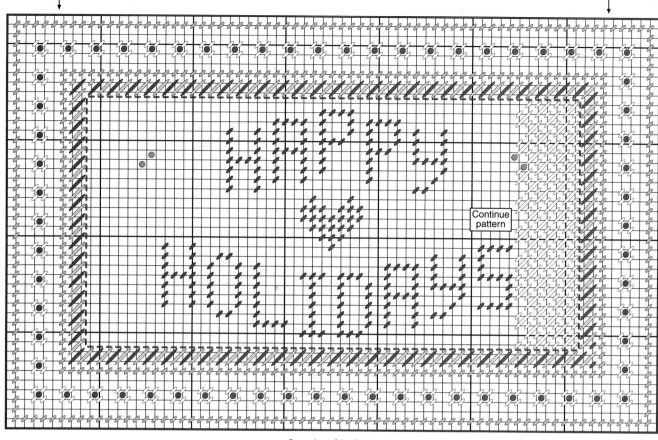

Greeting Girl Sign
70 holes x 43 holes
Cut 2, stitch 1

COLOR KEY	
Worsted Weight Yarn	**Yards**
☐ White #1	28
■ Black #12	2
☐ Yellow #230	5
☐ Mid brown #339	5
■ Coffee #365	12
☐ Emerald green #676	20
■ Forest green #689	10
☐ Lily pink #719	2
■ Soft navy #853	10
■ Cherry red #912	25
Uncoded areas on dog are cornmeal #220 Continental Stitches	10
Uncoded areas on sign border are soft navy #853 Continental Stitches	
⁄ Cornmeal #220 Whipstitching	
⁄ Black #12 Straight Stitch	
⁄ Mid brown #339 Backstitch and Straight Stitch	
⁄ Cherry red #912 Backstitch and Straight Stitch	
● Cherry red #912 French Knot	
△ Mid brown #339 Lark's Head Knot	
○ White #1 Turkey Loop Stitch	
◉ Mid brown #339 Turkey Loop Stitch	

Color numbers given are for Coats & Clark Red Heart Classic worsted weight yarn Art. E267.

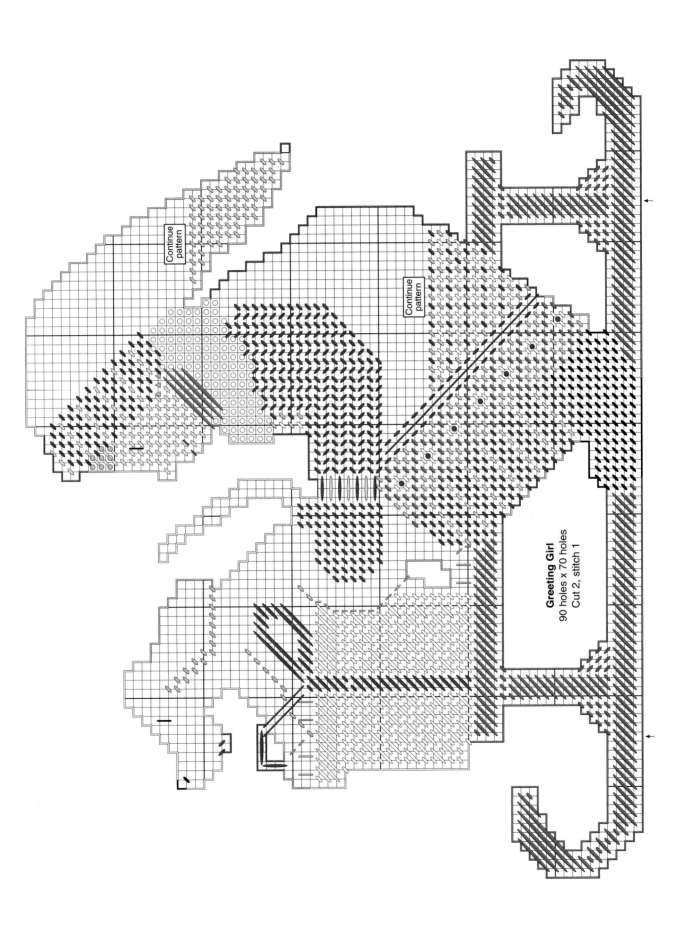

Continue pattern

Continue pattern

Greeting Girl
90 holes x 70 holes
Cut 2, stitch 1

Santa & the Mrs. Gift Totes

Designs by Kathleen Hurley

Stuff these reusable totes with cookies, candy or other holiday treats—they're really two gifts in one!

Skill Level

Beginner

Finished Size

4⅛ inches W x 5½ inches H, excluding handles

Materials

- 1½ sheets 7-count plastic canvas
- Coats & Clark Red Heart Classic worsted weight yarn Art. E267 as listed in color key
- 2 yards gold craft cord
- #16 tapestry needle

Instructions

1. Cut plastic canvas according to graphs. Cut one 26-hole x 6-hole piece for each tote bottom. Tote bottoms will remain unstitched.

2. Stitch and Overcast Santa and Mrs. Santa with Continental and Slanted Gobelin Stitches following graphs, working uncoded areas on Santa with jockey red Continental Stitches and uncoded areas on Mrs. Santa with sea coral Continental Stitches.

3. Using white, work two Straight Stitches per hole for Santa's mustache. Using 2 plies yarn, work all French Knots on faces, Santa and tree; work Straight Stitches for Mrs. Santa's mouth.

4. Stitch tote pieces following graphs, working one front and back set with forest green and white stripes, and remaining front and back set replacing forest green with cardinal.

5. Using white throughout, Overcast top edges of fronts, backs and sides. For each set, Whipstitch one front and back to two sides, then Whipstitch front, back and sides to unstitched bottom.

6. Cut craft cord into six 12-inch lengths. Thread one length through hole indicated at top of Christmas tree. Tie in a bow; trim ends as desired. Thread one length from back to front through two holes indicated with orange dots on Mrs. Santa. Tie in a bow; trim ends as desired.

7. Use photo as a guide through step 8. For handles, along top edge in the sixth hole from corners on each front and back piece, thread ends of one length of craft cord from outside to inside, knotting ends on inside of bag.

8. Center and glue Santa to front of cardinal tote and Mrs. Santa to front of forest green tote, making sure bottom edges are even. ❄

COLOR KEY		
Worsted Weight Yarn		**Yards**
☐ White #1		36
■ Black #12		2
☐ Yellow #230		1
☐ Sea coral #246		2
▨ Warm brown #336		1
▨ Silver #412		1
☐ Paddy green #686		4
▨ Forest green #689		13
☐ Pink #737		1
☐ Light periwinkle #827		2
■ Jockey red #902		7
▨ Cherry red #912		1
Cardinal #917		12
Uncoded areas on Mrs. Santa are sea coral #246 Continental Stitches		
Uncoded areas on Santa are jockey red #902 Continental Stitches		
⟋ White #1 Straight Stitch		
⟋ Jockey red #902 Straight Stitch		
○ White #1 French Knot		
○ Yellow #230 French Knot		
○ Pink #737 French Knot		
○ Light periwinkle #827 French Knot		
● Jockey red #902 French Knot		
Color numbers given are for Coats & Clark Red Heart Classic worsted weight yarn Art. E267.		

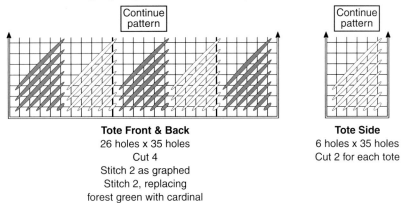

Tote Front & Back
26 holes x 35 holes
Cut 4
Stitch 2 as graphed
Stitch 2, replacing
forest green with cardinal

Tote Side
6 holes x 35 holes
Cut 2 for each tote

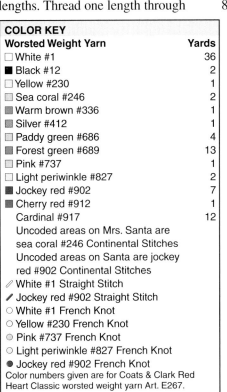

Tote Mrs. Santa
21 holes x 35 holes
Cut 1

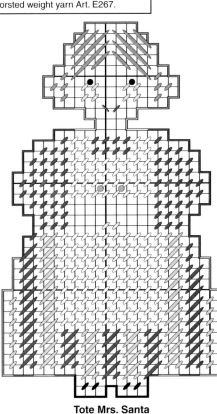

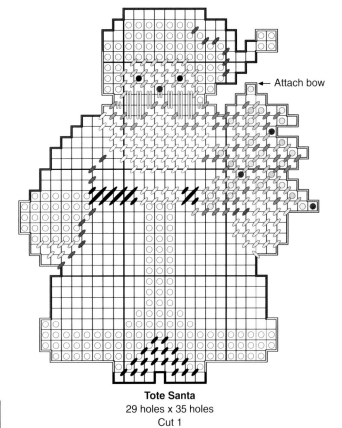

← Attach bow

Tote Santa
29 holes x 35 holes
Cut 1

Snowman & Wreath Garland

Design by Judy Collishaw

Plump snowmen holding cheerful red-and-green wreaths are sure to lift your spirits during the winter months!

Skill Level

Beginner

Finished Size

33¼ inches W x 4¼ inches H, excluding hangers

Materials

- 2 sheets 7-count plastic canvas
- Worsted weight yarn as listed in color key
- #16 tapestry needle
- Low-temperature glue gun

Instructions

1. Cut plastic canvas according to graphs.

2. Stitch and Overcast pieces following graphs, working uncoded areas on snowmen with white Continental Stitches.

3. When background stitching and Overcasting are completed, work eyes, nose, mouth and buttons with 2 plies yarn. Work French Knots on wreaths with 3 plies red.

4. Using photo as a guide and using green yarn, attach hands of snowmen to wreaths where indicated on graphs with arrows. Thread an 8-inch length of green yarn through top hole of hands at each end of garland; tie yarn ends together in a knot to form a loop for hanging.

5. Glue hats to heads at an angle. Glue bows to bottoms of wreaths. ✳

COLOR KEY

Worsted Weight Yarn	Yards
▨ Kelly green	15
■ Red	12
▨ Brown	5
Uncoded areas on snowmen are white Continental Stitches	26
⁄ White Overcasting	
╱ Black Backstitch	6
● Orange Straight Stitch	1
● Red French Knot	
● Black French Knot	

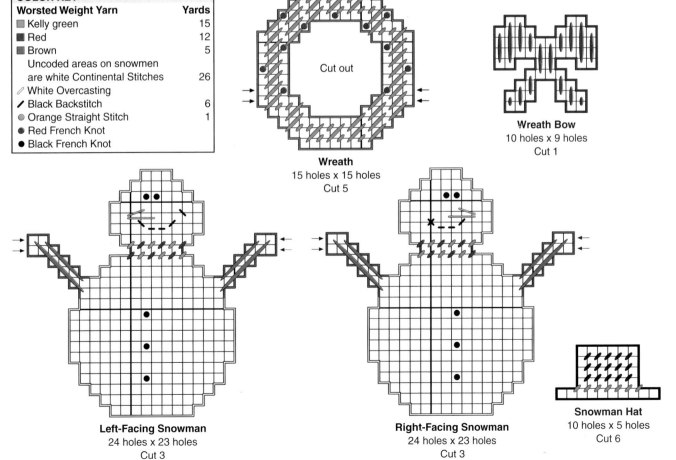

Cut out

Wreath
15 holes x 15 holes
Cut 5

Wreath Bow
10 holes x 9 holes
Cut 1

Left-Facing Snowman
24 holes x 23 holes
Cut 3

Right-Facing Snowman
24 holes x 23 holes
Cut 3

Snowman Hat
10 holes x 5 holes
Cut 6

Christmas Joy **185**

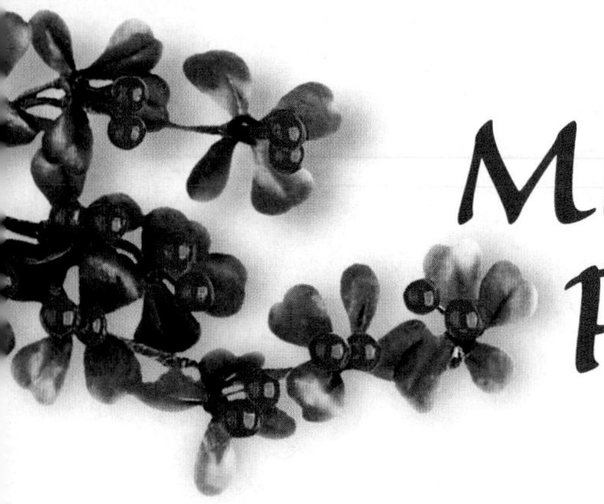

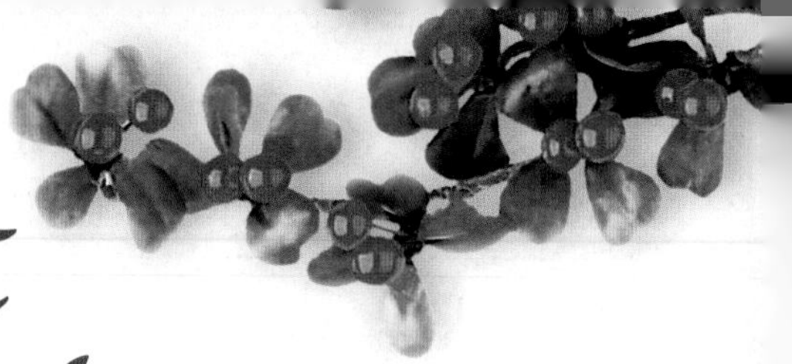

Midnight Poinsettias

Design by Kathleen Hurley

Elegant poinsettias will look right at home during your most formal holiday entertaining. Change the background to soft white for a more casual look—beautiful either way!

Skill Level

Beginner

Finished Size

Fits boutique-style tissue box

Materials

- 1½ sheets 7-count plastic canvas
- Coats & Clark Red Heart Classic worsted weight yarn Art. E267 as listed in color key
- #16 tapestry needle

Instructions

1. Cut plastic canvas according to graphs.

2. Stitch cover sides and top following graphs, working uncoded areas with black Continental Stitches and working two stitches per hole where indicated for borders on top piece.

3. Using black throughout, Overcast inside edges of top and bottom edges of sides. Whipstitch sides together, then Whipstitch sides to top. ❄

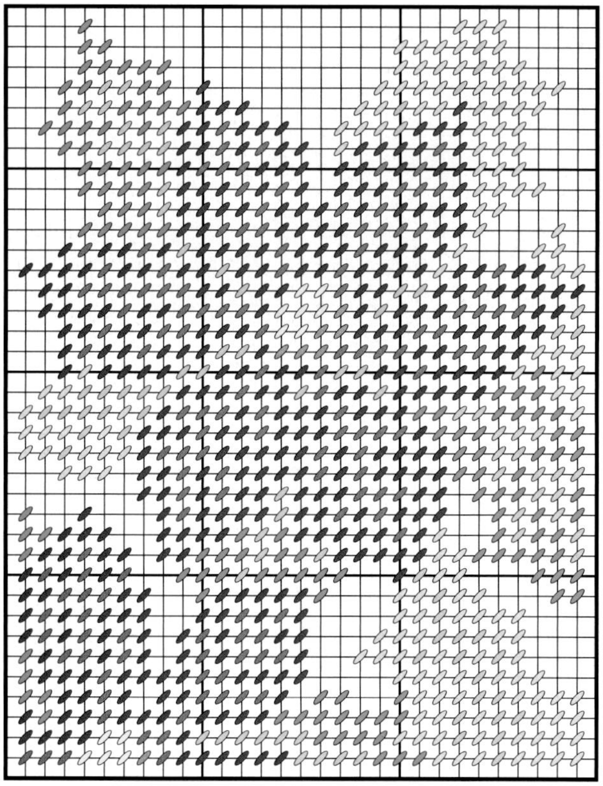

Midnight Poinsettias Cover Side
30 holes x 38 holes
Cut 4

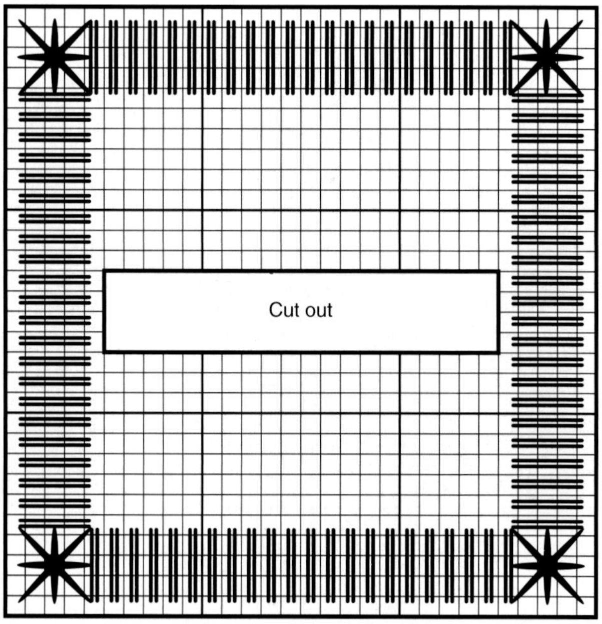

Midnight Poinsettias Cover Top
30 holes x 30 holes
Cut 1

COLOR KEY	
Worsted Weight Yarn	**Yards**
■ Black #12	41
□ Yellow #230	2
■ Orange #245	2
□ Emerald green #676	10
■ Paddy green #686	12
□ Forest green #689	8
■ Jockey red #902	22
■ Cherry red #912	10
Uncoded areas are black #12 Continental Stitches	

Color numbers given are for Coats & Clark Red Heart Classic worsted weight yarn Art. E267.

Stitch Guide

Use the following diagrams to expand your plastic canvas stitching skills. For each diagram, bring needle up through canvas at the red number one and go back down through the canvas at the red number two. The second stitch is numbered in green. Always bring needle up through the canvas at odd numbers and take it back down through the canvas at the even numbers.

Background Stitches

The following stitches are used for filling in large areas of canvas. The Continental Stitch is the most commonly used stitch. Other stitches, such as the Condensed Mosaic and Scotch Stitch, fill in large areas of canvas more quickly than the Continental Stitch because their stitches cover a larger area of canvas.

Continental Stitch

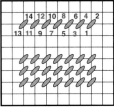

Condensed Mosaic

Alternating Continental

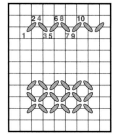

Cross Stitch

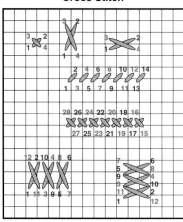

Long Stitch

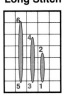

Slanted Gobelin

Scotch Stitch

Embroidery Stitches

These stitches are worked on top of a stitched area to add detail to the project. Embroidery stitches are usually worked with one strand of yarn, several strands of pearl cotton or several strands of embroidery floss.

Lattice Stitch

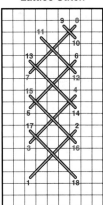

Chain Stitch

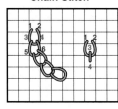

Couching

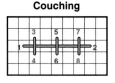

Straight Stitch

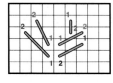

Running Stitch

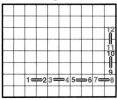

Fly Stitch

Backstitch

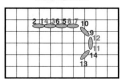

Embroidery Stitches

French Knot

Bring needle up through canvas.

Wrap yarn around needle 1 to 3 times, depending on desired size of knot; take needle back through canvas through same hole.

Lazy Daisy

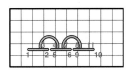

Loop Stitch or Turkey Loop Stitch

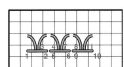

Bring yarn needle up through canvas, then back down in same hole, leaving a small loop.

Then, bring needle up inside loop; take needle back down through canvas on other side of loop.

The top diagram shows this stitch left intact. This is an effective stitch for giving a project dimensional hair. The bottom diagram demonstrates the cut loop stitch. Because each stitch is anchored, cutting it will not cause the stitches to come out. A group of cut loop stitches gives a fluffy, soft look and feel to your project.

Specialty Stitches

The following stitches can be worked either on top of a previously stitched area or directly onto the canvas. Like the embroidery stitches, these too add wonderful detail and give your stitching additional interest and texture.

Diamond Eyelet

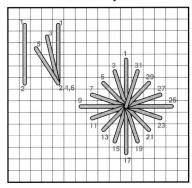

For each stitch, bring needle up at odd numbers and down through canvas at center hole.

Smyrna Cross

Satin Stitches

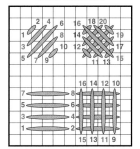

This stitch gives a "padded" look to your work.

Finishing Stitches

Overcast/Whipstitch

Overcasting and Whipstitching are used to finish the outer edges of the canvas. Overcasting is done to finish one edge at a time. Whipstitch is used to stitch two or more pieces of canvas together along an edge. For both Overcasting and Whipstitching, work one stitch in each hole along straight edges and inside corners, and two or three stitches in outside corners.

Lark's Head Knot

The Lark's Head Knot is used for a fringe edge or for attaching a hanging loop.

Special Thanks

We would like to acknowledge and thank the following designers whose original work has been published in this collection. We appreciate and value their creativity and dedication to designing quality plastic canvas projects!

Angie Arickx
Cardinal Snow Scene, Christmas Home Tissue Topper, Snowflake Cornices, Snowflake Quilt Block Set, Snow People, Snowy Brick Cottage

Jana Britton
Holly Basket, Snow Girl Dress-Up Doll, Wild West Snowman

Ronda Bryce
Cozy Coaster-Chair Set, Snow Family

Judy Collishaw
Caroling Penguin, It's Snow Time!, Snow-Happy Note Holder, Snowman & Snow Lady, Snowman & Wreath Garland

Nancy Dorman
Birdseed Snowman, Snowy Cardinal

Susan D. Fisher
Snowman With Heart

Janelle Giese
Candy Cane Friends, Quilted Snowman, Santa Canister

Joan Green
Beaded Snowflakes, Jeweled Snowflake, Peppermint Snowman Advent Calendar, Snow Cat

Angels, Snow Chef, Snowflake Joy, Snowflake Reflections, Snowman Pillow Appliqué, Snowman Quilt, Snowy Golf Buddies, Snowy Lodge Coaster Set, Snowy Trees & Snowman

Kathleen Hurley
Penguin Coaster, Midnight Poinsettias, Mini Candy Cup, Santa & the Mrs. Gift Totes, Santa's Coming Stocking, Snowman & Cardinals

Carol Krob
Mitten Garland

Christina Laws
Christmas Paper Roll Holders

Susan Leinberger
Folk-Art Greeting Girl, Signs of Christmas, Smiling Snowman Purse, Snowman Suncatcher

Valerie Leinberger
Silly Snowman Ornament

Lee Lindeman
Chubby Angel & Santa, Eskimo Shadow Box, Jolly Santa, Penguin Pals, Winter Friends

Kristine Loffredo
Doves in Pine, Kitty & Pup Treat Holders, Winter Cardinals

Alida Macor
Gift Mittens

Nancy Marshall
Sitting Snowman

Jocelyn Sass and Karen White of Creatively Sassy
Snowmen Peg Rack, Snowman Towel Holder

Kimberly A. Suber
Snowman for Hire

Marianne Telesca
Snowflake Basket

Ruby Thacker
Snowflake Shapes

Vickery Designs
Christmas Glass Cozies

Laura Victory
Clay Pot Snowmen

Michele Wilcox
Sledding Snowman Doorstop

Kathy Wirth
Frosted Snowflakes, Hot Chocolate Set, Juggling Snowman, Layered Snowflake Frame, Sledding Fun, Snowman Wind Chime

Buyer's Guide

When looking for a specific material, first check your local craft and retail stores. If you are unable to locate a product locally, contact the manufacturers listed below for the closest retail source in your area or a mail-order source.

Amaco
American Art Clay Co. Inc.
4717 W. 16th St.
Indianapolis, IN 46222-2598
(317) 244-6871
www.amaco.com

The Beadery
P.O. Box 178
Hope Valley, RI 02832
(401) 539-2432

Caron International
P.O. Box 222
Washington, NC 27889
www.caron.com

Coats & Clark
Consumer Service
P.O. Box 12229
Greenville, SC 29612-0229
(800) 648-1479
www.coatsandclark.com

Daniel Enterprises
P.O. Box 1105
Laurinburg, NC 28353
(910) 277-7441

Darice
Mail-order source:
Schrock's International
P.O. Box 538
Bolivar, OH 44612
(330) 874-3700

Designs by Joan Green
P.O. Box 715
Oxford, OH 45056
(513) 523-0437
(Mon.–Fri., 9 a.m.–5 p.m.)

DMC Corp.
Hackensack Ave. Bldg. 10A
South Kearny, NJ 07032-4688
(800) 275-4117
www.dmc-usa.com

Elmore-Pisgah Inc.
P.O. Box 187
Spindale, NC 28160
(828) 286-3665

Fibre-Craft Materials Corp.
Mail-order source:
Kirchen Brothers
P.O. Box 1016
Skokie, IL 60076
(800) 378-5024
e-mail: kirchenbro@aol.com

FloraCraft Corp.
P.O. Box 400
Ludington, MI 49431
(231) 845-5127
www.floracraft.com

Forster Inc./Diamond Brands
800 Cloquet Ave.
Cloquet, MN 55720
(218) 879-6700

Gay Bowles Sales Inc.
P.O. Box 1060
Janesville, WI 53547
(800) 447-1332
www.millhill.com

Hot Off The Press Inc.
1250 N.W. Third
Canby, OR 97013
(888) 326-7255
www.hotp.com

Kreinik Mfg. Co. Inc.
3106 Timanus Ln., #101
Baltimore, MD 21244-2871
(800) 537-2166

Kunin Felt Co./Foss Mfg. Co. Inc.
P.O. Box 5000
Hampton, NH 03843-5000
(603) 929-6100
www.kuninfelt.com

Lion Brand Yarn Co.
34 W. 15th St.
New York, NY 10011
(800) 795-5466

Plaid Enterprises Inc.
3225 Westech Dr.
Norcross, Ga 30092
(800) 842-4197
www.plaidonline.com

Rainbow Gallery
Mail-order source:
Designs by Joan Green
P.O. Box 715
Oxford, OH 45056
(513) 523-0437
(Mon.–Fri., 9 a.m.–5 p.m.)

Sonburn
P.O. Box 167
Addison, TX 75001
(800) 527-7505
www.sonburn.com

Uniek
Mail-order source:
Annie's Attic
1 Annie Ln.
Big Sandy, TX 75755
(800) 582-6643
www.anniesattic.com

Walnut Hollow Farm Inc.
1409 State Rd. 23
Dodgeville, WI 53533-2112
(800) 950-5101
www.walnuthollow.com

Westrim Crafts/Western Trimming Corp.
9667 Canoga Ave.
P.O. Box 3879
Chatsworth, CA 91311
(818) 998-8550

Wimpole Street Creations
Mail-order source:
Barrett House
P.O. Box 540585
North Salt Lake, UT 84054-0585
(801) 299-0700
www.barrett-house.com

Notes